HOW CAN YOU BELIEVE?

FOR THOSE WHO SEEK

George W. Wickersham II

Foreword by Sydney Evans

R.B.S. 3/3/04

from Fannie R – 3/3/93

CHURCHMAN PUBLISHING

How Can You Believe?
by
George W. Wickersham II
was first published in 1989 by
Churchman Publishing Limited
117 Broomfield Avenue
Worthing, West Sussex BN14 7SF

Publisher: Peter Smith

Represented in
Dublin; Sydney; Wellington;
Kingston, Ontario and Wilton, Connecticut

Distributed to the book trade by
Bailey Book Distribution Limited
(a division of the Bailey and Swinfen Holdings Group)
Warner House, Wear Bay Road,
Folkestone, Kent CT19 6PH

ISBN 1 85093 122 4

Printed in Great Britain by
Dotesios Printers Limited, Trowbridge, Wiltshire.

FOREWORD

If you really are searching for a faith to live by; or if you are needing a fresh look at the faith by which you are already living; if you do not find the assumptions of an acquisitive society a satisfying interpretation of the mystery and meaning of being alive and being human, then read this book.

You will not find here complicated arguments or words you've never met before. Rather you will find yourself being led step by step through the sort of questions you've often asked yourself or heard others asking in the search for life's meaning. You will find yourself being led by a writer who speaks to you directly and goes along with you as a companion. He's been travelling this way during a long life, but he writes with the fresh eagerness of a young man who has glimpsed a vision that he feels impelled to share with others. He tells the unique story that has Jesus at its centre and faces the questions this story raises for those who hear it at the end of the twentieth century.

So, if you are baffled by the Bible and by the painful contradictions of human experience; if you doubt the existence of any Reality which can meaningfully be addressed as God, you will be helped to distinguish between fact and interpretation, between history and metaphor, between prose and poetry. You will be encouraged to open your mind and heart afresh to quotations from Hebrew and Christian literature that still glow with the light of deep wisdom.

SYDNEY EVANS

Dean Emeritus of Salisbury and

former Dean of King's College London.

To my wife

"Pie"

usually known as "Betty"

*who patiently listened
to the formulation of
each chapter and then
made suggestions which
were always right.*

TABLE OF CONTENTS

PREFACE

ALL of the biblical quotations in this book are taken from the Revised Standard Version of 1952, except where otherwise noted. The major exception to this rule is found in connection with the Psalms. The quotes from this collection of beautiful utterances are taken from the "Great Bible" translation of 1539, as revised for the (American) Book of Common Prayer of 1928. Since the Psalms are poetry, it seemed logical to use what I consider to be the most poetic of English translations.

The reader will find all quotes footnoted. My suggestion is to ignore the little numbers, unless one has a special interest in looking up a particular reference. There are but few other types of footnotes in the book, and running the eye (and the hand) to the end of the chapter is apt to break the chain of thought.

The question from which comes the title of this work was asked by Wendy. I am indebted to her for setting the book in motion, albeit some twenty-five years before I actually took pen in hand. I trust that she will forgive me for being so long with it.

G.W.W.II

Rockbridge Baths, Virginia

PROLOGUE

EXPRESSED in many different forms, the question, "How can you believe?", implies that there are serious barriers to accepting belief in the existence of God, let alone the basic Christian credo that Jesus is Lord. But the barriers, so often, appear to be tied to lesser questions. Enquirers are apt to ask, "In order to be a Christian do I have to believe all that other stuff: the Old Testament God? the devil? hell? the infallible Bible?"

It is easy enough to say "No!" to all such queries, and to let it go at that, but people hear of all of these things continually, both in church and out, and simply find them too hot to handle.

I have often heard it said that if you want to convert someone to Christianity the best thing that you can do is to give her or him a Bible. As far as I am concerned, that is probably the worst thing that you can do.

I remember a young person in one of my groups telling us how he had resolved to read the Bible from cover to cover, but when he got to the dreadful doings of some of the Old Testament heroes, he was revolted, and when he got to the Law and its inexplicable and often ugly demands, he was utterly repelled. He quickly gave up his project. Alas, he has much company.

Even the New Testament presents difficulties: John's contradictions of Matthew, Mark and Luke, Peter's and Paul's male chauvinism, Paul's rabbinical reasoning and the vengeful God of the Book of Revelation.

Sunday School materials, almost uniformly, close their collective eyes to these obstacles, and teach our children that the Bible is "The Word of God." Old Testament heroes are presented minus their sins, the Law is confined to the Ten Commandments and the contradictions in the New Testament are glossed over. All of this is usually sugar-coated with denominational formularies and fetishes of which the first Christians never even thought. This process is bound to lead to subsequent disillusionment.

To me, the Bible is indeed the Word of God, but it is the Word of God in the words of people - people as fallible as all people are. Perused with this in mind, the Bible becomes a very different volume. Thus viewed, it becomes a totally fascinating compilation of works. And why? It is the one anthology which clearly shows what the idea of one God, who is righteous, led to. One might well add that it also shows, in sometimes lurid hues, what it led from. More than that, it records, at least so I believe, what that one God said and did when he saw fit to visit this planet. What more could one ask?

Of course the Bible presents difficulties. Again, it was written by people: people like you and me. The major purpose of this work is to point out that, all of this notwithstanding, the Scriptures do indeed justify themselves - indeed, more than that. Through all the dross and drudgery of much of the Old Testament, God's influence does become peculiarly evident. It is as though he were always endeavoring to draw people to himself. Like headstrong children, people either rebelled or misunderstood, but again like other children, some yielded to parental influence and did in time become "strong in the Lord." In fact, not a few became lights to their generations and to all generations. God did break through the human barrier. To discover these "breaks" in the Old Testament and to glory in them is now our privilege.

In the New Testament we find startling evidence of a divine visitation. Of course it is confused and somewhat self-contradictory. What else could one reasonably expect it to be? But it is still irresistible. The majesty of its books is more than sufficient evidence of a cataclysmic event. The same God whom we saw at work in the Old Testament comes alive in Jesus of Nazareth. This is the God who bore with people and all of their many sins (set forth so impartially in the Old Book), the God who led people on to an ever-deepening understanding of his nature, the God of "stedfast love." In the New Book we read of that love having its ultimate expression in the very death of the Lord himself: the most amazing story in all history - and the most moving: the God who dies.

Actually, the whole Bible is nothing more than the parable of the prodigal son writ large. God is the father, humanity, the son. The parable continues down to the present moment, and will continue until the end of time. The text for this mortal life might well be found in the words of the Master, "Come to me, all who labor and are heavy-laden, and I will give you rest."[1] Forgiveness is wholesale; in fact, it is totally free of charge. The price of stedfast love has been fully paid. What else is the meaning of the cross?

The barriers to believing this are contained in our own condition. Evidences of this are also writ large in both books. So how do we separate the true from the not-so-true? How do we evaluate the Scriptures? The key is actually simple: it is the remembrance of love. "God is love,"[2] wrote St. John. Whatever else St. John wrote, or anyone else wrote, should be evaluated on that basis.

In a society which must necessarily be based largely on human nature - the very reverse of love - it was and still is extremely difficult not to warp "the Word of God" as it comes to us from above. Charges are added to forgiveness. From this simple fact arise the major barriers to a reasonable Christian belief: the vengeful God, hell, male chauvinism, the strident claims of inerrancy, etc., not to mention all the denominational rules, regulations and rivalries of the so-called "Christian era." These are not "the Word of God" at all. They are the words of humanity.

With care and with thought, all of these barriers to a thoughtful conviction can, I am convinced, be broken down. To do exactly that, and to do it piece by piece, is the purpose of this book.

It is also the purpose of this book to present an acceptable foundation to that basic assumption that there is a God to begin with. Both the Old and the New Testaments stand, I hold, as sufficient evidence that there is a Deity, and we bear down on this point. Still, nobody can escape the need for that ultimate source of conviction: experience. We bear down on this also, and endeavor to throw light on this crucial matter.

It was the father of a young epileptic who cried out and said to Jesus, "I believe; help my unbelief!"[3] I dare say that he spoke for millions, including me. I hope that this work will be of help precisely along those lines.

NOTES

1. Matthew 11:28
2. I John 4:8 and 16
3. Mark 11:24

I

HOW CAN YOU BELIEVE?

"HOW CAN YOU BELIEVE that there is a God?" The question was put by a thirteen-year old girl at a meeting of a young people's group in one of my various parishes.

The youth fellowship of a church may be of some benefit to the young people, but I am inclined to think that it is of more benefit to its adult leaders. This is because children tend to call a spade a spade. They have not gotten into the morass of adult self-deception. Thus their leaders often find themselves embarrassed and squirming - and thinking.

"How can you believe that there is a God?" How indeed? In the adult world such a question is usually avoided. Not only does it tend to raise differences of opinion, but also it usually intrudes upon carefully guarded illusions. Most people want to believe in something, and perhaps - just perhaps - there is nothing. Many parents, I am sure, try to teach their children to believe in God when they themselves have grave doubts about him.

Children are inclined to accept their parents' word on things of this sort and to go along with it, at least until they begin to sense their parents' own uncertainties and inconsistencies. Sooner or later the day of reckoning arrives. For some young people it arrives in junior high, for others, not until university. Many young people toss their childish acceptances out the window at the first onslaught of a doubting teacher or an agnostic book. Others wrestle valiantly with philosophy and theology until they come to a reasoned point of view one way or the other. Still others learn their parents' tricks of sublimating the process of thinking. For them even Santa Claus remains at least a remote possibility.

All of which represents only the beginning of the answer to that searching question, "How can you believe that there is a God?"

A non-swimmer, standing by the river, finds it difficult to accept the idea that he can swim in its clear green waters. Even the sight of others enjoying the cool pleasure of the stream does not reassure the novice. A little instruction, a little help - these go a long way, but ultimately one has to wade in to find out. So it is with belief in God. There is no getting around the act of faith. Belief in God ultimately requires the experience of him. "Behold, I stand at the door and knock," the Lord is quoted in Revelation; "if any one hears my voice and opens the door, I will come in to him..."[1] The proof of the pudding, invariably, is in the eating.

Occasionally we see a child take his parents at their word to the point of making the act of faith, even when they never have. The young person does actually open the door, and God quite evidently does become real to her or to him. This is a phenomenon of considerable interest and can result in some rather amazing displays of character. A committed young person is always a source of wonder and gratification, even to the uncommitted. The demon of "peer pressure," which seems inevitably to be aimed in the wrong direction, is peremptorily slain. This can happen and it should, far more often than we expect it to. Indeed, if our expectations were higher, so would be the occurrences.

Be that as it may, at the very best it is only a start. One of the most sobering incidents in my youth took place in England on the path approaching Salisbury Cathedral. A college friend and I were walking to service there. An erect and seasoned gentleman caught up with us and asked if we were Americans. Yes, we were Americans. "Do you always go to church?" Yes, we did. "Extraordinary!" he exclaimed. "You Americans accept everything on faith. Me - I had to go through the coffee mill to discover that there is a God!" He doffed his hat at the mention of the sacred name and disappeared into the soaring nave of that sublime edifice.

During the years which have followed that startling encounter I have come to the realization that nobody, whether believing or unbelieving, can fully escape that coffee mill.

Most of us begin life thinking of ourselves very highly indeed, which may be just as well. It takes some years to discover the truth. Some there are who never discover it, or at least never face it. These latter die in the terror and exhaustion of constant flight. Nor should we condemn them. The rest of us, for the most part, have also done our share of running away. And why not? The truth about us is, I fear, something from which to flee. For the truth is that none of us really amounts to very much. The parable of the Pharisee and the publican is on the mark. The man who "would not even lift up his eyes to heaven, but beat his breast, saying, ' God be merciful to me a sinner!'"[2] was the one who had actually faced himself.

Who will deny it? We are vain, insensitive, irritable, impatient, unforgiving, moody, critical, envious, jealous, lazy, defensive, self-seeking, self-indulgent, self-centered. We are filled with anger, violence and all manner of inordinate affections. Caprice, compromise, capitulation - these lie at the heart of human nature. The very term, "human nature," carries derogatory implications. The General Confession of the Book of Common Prayer, whether said weekly or daily, always applies: "We have left undone those things which we ought to have done; and we have done those things which we ought not to have done; *and there is no health in us*." Until we are capable of admitting this and of crying out for help, the coffee mill grinds on.

And what is this coffee mill? For the answer to this question we might well turn to the third chapter of Genesis. Whatever one may think of that ancient book, it does have rather telling insights into questions which have long intrigued our race. One such question has been the troublesome life of the human animal, as opposed the apparent care-free attitude of the rest of the world's creatures. Why should we not continue in a Garden of Eden, "doing what comes naturally"? Genesis pins the blame on the knowledge of good and evil. From the time that our forebears gained this sensibility, the Garden of Eden was finished. Life was no longer simply a matter of fulfilling one's instincts. Suddenly there were moral issues. Worse than that, the basic self-centeredness of a person's life was recognized, and every human being found herself or himself burdened with guilt. The coffee mill had commenced to grind.

"I do not understand my own actions," St. Paul wrote to the Romans, "for I do not do what I want, but I do the very thing I hate."[3] St. Paul also speaks of "dying in Adam."[4] This is an apt expression, for with the knowledge which, according to Genesis, we obtained in Adam when he and Eve ate the fruit (not an apple!), we become aware of the unappealing condition of our souls. The knowledge of evil elicits the emotion of disgust. Yet with all this we are unaware of any power with which to change ourselves. The coffee mill! Our illusions of grandeur are ground to powder.

No wonder that people become addicted to props, and some to props from which they never awaken. How can we respect ourselves? Where is self-esteem? "Wretched man that I am!" cries St. Paul. "Who will deliver me from this body of death?"[5]

The story of human travail begins in the Book of Genesis. It ends in the Revelation to St. John the Divine. Between these two we read the majestic story of the redemption of humanity - for God not only gave his children the knowledge of good and evil, he also gave them himself.

The patriarchs and prophets of the Old Testament discovered that the Lord God was at hand: Abraham at Mamre, Jacob at Jabbok, Moses at the Bush, Elijah at Horeb, Isaiah, Amos, Hoseah, Jeremiah, the psalmists - the list is long. "Seek the Lord while he may be found, call upon him while he is near."[6] Then follows the matchless testimony of the New Testament: "Come to me, all who labor and are heavy-laden, and I will give you rest."[7]

Herein lies the one possible escape from the coffee mill. Alcoholics who have hitherto doubted the existence of God find themselves caught between the specter of alcoholic death on the one hand and the prospect of help from a higher power on the other. They know that they cannot achieve sobriety on their own. Even the help of fellow sufferers is not enough. The ultimate strength to get well is available only from the invisible source to which we attach the name, "God."

This is but an inevitable ramification of the fact that without the help of the Almighty you cannot overcome yourself, your passions and your essentially selfish impulses: you cannot reach that halcyon state wherein you can respect yourself. Self-esteem is impossible.

How can you believe that there is a God? Life is long and daily. No matter who you are or what your point of view, life grinds out the same lesson slowly, ceaselessly, irresistibly. Not everyone is willing to face it, but there it is. We are sinners and we know it. Pride alone prevents our admitting it.

If we rely on our own powers and seek to achieve respectability by ourselves, we begin to see the growth of that sophisticated hypocrite which so many people actually are. This process, essentially one of self-deception, takes place easily enough, but becomes more and more unendurable as time goes on. Our sins: "The remembrance of them is grievous unto us; The burden of them is intolerable."[8] The coffee mill grinds fine.

There is, as far as I know, only one workable alternative. That is to reach out for the unseen hand. If we do, then we reverse the usual process. As we grow in age, we grow in grace and in that Christlike stature to which all ultimately aspire. The proof of the pudding is indeed in the eating.

This is how most earnest believers come to the conviction that there is a God. It is not primarily an intellectual process. Belief emerges, usually over a period of time, out of a desperate struggle in the soul.

We do not see God, we do not hear him, but if we ask to be changed, we are.

NOTES

1. Revelation 3:20
2. Luke 18:10-14
3. Romans 7:15
4. 1 Corinthians 15:22
5. Romans 7:24
6. Isaiah 55:6
7. Matthew 11:28
8. General Confession for Holy Communion, Book of Common Prayer

II

ADAM'S DESCENDANTS - BAD?

THE SELF-CENTEREDNESS of human nature is not the result of a miscalculation made by the Creator, nor is it the residue of some sort of spiritual disease inherited from Adam and Eve. It is exactly what one would expect of a creature who is, to all intents and purposes, free.

If the New Testament says anything, it says that human beings are made for love: love between God and them, love between themselves. But love is not love if it is not voluntary. It must be offered "from the heart." This requires freedom of choice. The New Testament is actually based on this point. The coming of the Christ into the world as a human being with human limitations clearly implies that the Creator will never trespass on our right to choose. Jesus exemplified a certain nature. Either we respond to him or we do not. Had the gracious words of God been written in fiery letters in the firmament, and been repeated periodically, there would be little doubt as to what the situation is. More than that, there would be considerable pressure to comply. But of the man from Nazareth we can always say that he was just a man, albeit a good one, and of the accounts in the Gospels, we can always say that they are exaggerations. There is no pressure.

In any event, it is a recognizable fact that Jesus did not come down from the cross, and also that, as he himself insisted would be the case, no "sign" was given to his detractors. (Of this, more in later chapters.) The point being that freedom is of the essence of a humanity which the Deity woos to be his devoted family. But such a freedom, aside from its unspeakable cost to the Creator, carries a cost to us, and this is the item which is so frequently overlooked.

The price of freedom is self-centeredness. How can it be otherwise? If there are no strings attached to you, and none to me, then you are at the center of your world, and I, at the center of mine. As far as you are concerned, the world goes around you, and as far as I am concerned, it goes around me. This does not necessarily imply enmity, but it does leave each one of us "locked in" to separate worlds. Enmity comes all too quickly when our interests conflict. It is, I fear, "only natural" that we should, as some wag remarked, "do unto others before they do unto us."

Into this situation we who call ourselves Christians throw the idea that people are made for love. In view of the above, this sounds like an about-face. However, anyone who has had experience with little ones knows how a squalling, totally self-concerned infant can be changed into an apparent angel by a little "tender loving care." So many examples come to mind: the child screaming in a restaurant, then totally charmed by a kind-hearted stranger; the frantic little lost one in a super-market falling in love with the policeman who rescues her. The embittered old man transformed by sincere attention. Who has not witnessed such?

Love most definitely lures us from our little personal worlds and does turn us around 180 degrees; not always, but often. From self-centered persons we become self-giving ones. Precisely here is perhaps the most important fact of human life: it takes love to elicit love. Indeed, it is one of the doctrines of current psychiatry that no one can love until she or he has been loved.

All of which raises a theological question - another crucial question usually overlooked: If human beings are incapable of originating love, whence came this precious item? So often the quick answer to this question is, "from one's parents." But this only pushes the answer farther back in time, for parents are also human beings and also incapable of originating love.

Most parents are capable of instinctive love of their offspring, but instinctive love is a fragile item and simply will not hold up for long under the relentless pressure of one's little, self-centered monsters. Those who have watched mothers with children in department stores know full well the hostility, the anger, the urge to kill which often develops in the harassed parent: "No, you can't have it. No! I said No!" Screams, hits, louder screams...

A mama-bear is bad news to intruders who approach her cubs. She gives herself wholly, we are told, to raising and training the little bruins. "Here is love!" you say, until the day comes when she chases them up tall trees and then goes off and abandons them. How many human parents would emphatically endorse such a measure!

No, instinctive love is not the real thing, and is far from enough. The sort of devotion of which the Gospels and the Epistles speak (*agape*) just is not in us. We are free, yes, but, inevitably, we are also self-centered. When it comes to love, the Prayer Book collect succinctly sums it up: "We have no power of ourselves to help ourselves."[1]

This is the condition of humanity referred to in the previous chapter. Every Book of Common Prayer in the Anglican Communion until the latest American one covered this condition with a phrase in the General Confession for Morning and Evening Prayer: "There is no health in us." The

1979 book of the (American) Episcopal Church omitted it. Perhaps the thought was that the phrase was ambiguous. And yet, theologically, it may well have been one of the most important lines in the entire volume. Goodness is love, and all love is from God. St. John states it flatly, "Beloved, let us love one another, for love is of God, and he who loves is born of God...."[2] St. Paul disclaims all virtue: "I have been crucified with Christ," he writes to the Galatians; "it is no longer I who live, but Christ who lives in me."[3] To the Romans he is even more bold: "for I know that nothing good dwells within me, that is, in my flesh."[4] In a later epistle, St. John writes simply, "He who does good is of God."[5]

Jesus, himself, could hardly have been more direct: "Why do you call me good?" he asked the rich young man. *"No one is good but God alone."*[6] Indeed, it is amazing that Mark, who believed implicitly in the divinity of Jesus,[7] should have recorded this. But our amazement at this apparent contradiction has, I fear, tended to distract us from the point of what Jesus was saying, which was plainly that all goodness is from God. There is indeed no health in us.

We are, of course, dealing with the ancient and honorable doctrine of original sin. This doctrine takes various forms in various traditions. The most common interpretation of it is the one attributing humanity's tendency towards evil to Adam's and Eve's disobedience in the garden. This, to my mind, is a rather unsatisfactory explanation. Aside from its pin-pointing the principal difference between humans and their animal cousins (the knowledge of good and evil), it presents a point of view hardly satisfactory to many of us. One finds great difficulty, for instance, in accepting the idea that God did not want his children to have the knowledge of good and evil, and even greater difficulty in believing that he should have expelled them from Eden because he did not want them and their descendants to have eternal life. The Lord God is quoted as saying of Adam,

> *"And now, lest he put forth his hand and take also of the tree of life, and eat, and live for ever" - therefore the Lord God sent him forth from the Garden of Eden.*[8]

Further, we do not readily accede to the idea of God's punishing all for the sin of two, or, indeed, of his putting a curse on both male and female.[9] (Imagine!) This cuts clean across the entire Christian idea.

Truth is, the tale, while intriguing and highly useful in song and story, is nevertheless misleading, and has been the source of enormous controversy. An understanding of the human condition can be arrived at simply by considering the untoward side of freedom, namely, self-centeredness, coupled with the capacity to distinguish good from bad: we are free, and are therefore self-confined; we know good and evil, and are therefore self-condemned.

Here is exactly where religion begins, for if God is not doing what the New Testament says that he is, then the future of the race must indeed be short. In fact, I cannot believe that we would be here at all unless he does stand at the door of every human heart, be it the heart of an English Christian, a Russian Communist, an Indian Hindu, an Asian Muslim or a Chinese Bhuddist. God stands knocking at every door and, either in the conscious or in the subconscious, his knock is heard. Nobody is without him, nobody unaffected. Were this not so, the human race would have destroyed itself almost before it had gotten started. Even with the divine knock, it has troubles enough.

The Holy Spirit! To the extent that we respond to him, we are redeemed. For thus love enters the world, and to the measure that it does, just to that measure the world is redeemed. Those who, one way or another, respond- these actually hold the world together.

Adam's descendants - are they bad? I would be inclined to say, "Not really." They have extraordinary capacities. In fact, what they can do is almost unbelievable. In music, in art, in literature, in science, in all manner of pursuits, the human animal is a wonder of wonders, even in his or her own eyes, and, I trust, in God's also.

True, human beings are, of themselves, isolated one from another, and this can have some very unhappy results. But all that they need in order to break this isolation is to be loved - and to respond. The good news is that they are so loved. The bad news is that, being free and therefore unpredictable, they do not always respond, and thus many remain potentially destructive and essentially unhappy.

St. Paul put it superbly: "for as in Adam all die," he wrote to the Corinthians, "so also in Christ shall all be made alive."[10]

NOTES

1. Book of Common Prayer, II Lent (1662 and others)
2. 1 John 4:7
3. Galatians 2:20
4. Romans 7:18a
5. 3 John 11b
6. Mark 10:18
7. Mark 1:11
8. Genesis 3:22b
9. Genesis 3:14-19
10. 1 Corinthians 15:22

III

THE BIBLE - TRUE ?

"DO YOU BELIEVE in the historical accuracy of the Bible?" The question was posed by a man high in the hierarchy of a conservative denomination. The setting was a noted morning television show. The query was addressed with some heat to a seminarian of the same convention. The young man obviously did not so believe, but was embarrassed to say so lest he offend many of his future constituents. But the question, as far as this writer is concerned, was a stupid one. It was in exactly the same category as, "Do you believe in the historical accuracy of The New York Times?" Sometimes The Times has it right, sometimes not. Items often breathe implausibility. The truth comes out, as a rule, in due course.

So often people will confront us with the tired saw, "If you believe part of the Bible but not all, then you might as well throw it all out." How ridiculous! Supposing that we were to apply that principle to the reading of other histories, or, indeed, to the reading of other philosophical works. We would simply have to throw them all out. Accounts of the American Civil War differ considerably in their detailing of its various issues and events. Which do we believe? Preachers of the Gospel differ even more in their respective interpretations of the faith. Which do we buy?

The Lord, in his mercy, gave us brains. I assume that he meant for us to use them. The writers of the Old Testament and of the New also had brains - brains which they used to varying degrees. More important than that, they had freedom, as do we - freedom which they had no choice but to use, and upon which God never imposed. The point being that if it is true that God ultimately came to earth as a man, a man who went to the cross rather than give "a sign," then it is also true that nobody was ever "taken over," either before or since. No one was ever made a secretary or a microphone for the purposes of the Deity. He respects our freedom even at the cost of the cross.

The Bible was written by human beings, many of them fabulous human beings, yes, but all of them fallible. We have to read their writings with this in mind. As with all other books which we may pick up and read, so with the Bible there is no way that we can escape having to use our own judgment.

Truth is, the inerrancy slant, usually referred to as fundamentalism, is not only contrary in principle to the way in which the Creator deals with his children, but also tends to obscure the true nature of the Bible. If all passages are in fact the handiwork of the Almighty, inerrant and not subject to human judgment, then all passages can be thought of as having equal value. This confronts us with a God who, in the Book of Joshua, commands Joshua to slay men, women and children (and beasts!) in the land of Canaan,[1] but in the Gospel of Matthew commands us (through Jesus) to love our enemies.[2] In Second Kings we read of the prophet Elijah twice calling down fire from Heaven to consume the king's messengers,[3] but in Luke we find Jesus expressly forbidding the disciples to attempt such a thing: "for the Son of Man came not to destroy men's lives but to save them."[4] There are literally hundreds of such contrasting passages in "The Book". Are we supposed to accept them all as "the Word of God"?

In the great drama of the 1930's, "The Green Pastures," a play written from the point of view of uneducated slaves, God is presented as constantly frustrated by the sinfulness of his children. He tries every tactic that he can think of to straighten them out, the most stringent one of which is, of course, the flood. Nothing seems to work. Finally, he sends his Son.

Anyone who saw the play will remember the expression on the face of "de Lawd" when the angels came to tell him that his Son was being crucified. The heavenly host confidently expected him to throw thunderbolts at the offending parties and to send a posse of angels to rescue the Son. But the Father simply stood there, leaning on his roll-top desk, eyes cast down. He had finally learned: in order to deal with people, you have to bear with them. God had been educated.

The Old Testament is not one book. It is a series of books, written over a period of as much as 1500 years or more. What makes it great is the fact that from the very beginning its authors had hold of one unifying idea: there is but one God. True, the idea was almost always burdened with the thought that God was somehow the special possession of Israel, or vice versa, but exactly herein lay the making of an unplanned plot of unparalleled importance - a plot which unfolds as the books proceed. For in spite of his rather partial leanings, God is always thought of as demanding some sort of right action. This was the second and equal half of the unifying idea, and was never omitted from it.

Cain's murder of Abel,[5] the wickedness of those who perished in the flood,[6] the Sodomites[7] - all exemplified transgression of a moral code which was considered as absolute. The Ten Commandments[8] and the incredibly elaborate Levitical Code[9] served to indicate that the Hebrew

God, no matter how favorable to the Hebrew people, was still an ethically demanding Deity. Therefore the prophets fulminated not only against the tendency of their people to worship other gods (which appears to have been a constant) but also against their greed, their lust and their continual disregard for the poor.

It was inevitable that in the course of time the more thoughtful of these people should begin to wonder about the relationship of this righteous God with people other than Jews. In Isaiah we find a new note with regards to these alien people. The Lord is cited as saying to Israel: "Behold, you shall call nations that you know not, and nations that knew you not shall run to you, because of the Lord your God, and of the Holy One of Israel, for he has glorified you."[10]

God was still Israel's special property, but others would ultimately come to Israel. This was the seed. It remained buried a long time. The prophets had enough trouble with their own people to be concerned about others. They saw their nation torn to shreds by foreign neighbors and they attributed these disasters to the wrath of their own God. Still, this did not serve to endear their neighbors to them.

But suffering also tends to breed humility, and thoughtful souls must have sometimes wondered whether the House of David was the only house with which the Lord God was concerned. The Book of Jonah was slow in coming, but, inexorably, it came. This is a satire which shouts one point: God cares as much for Ninevites as he does for Hebrews. Jonah in no way wanted to preach to Gentiles. He was afraid that they might listen, repent and be accepted. When that was exactly what happened, he was angry. But God rebuked him for his anger: "And should not I pity Nineveh, that great city, in which there are more than a hundred and twenty thousand persons who do not know their right hand from their left, and also much cattle?"[11]

Israel was indeed like Jonah, even to the point of being like Jonah in the big fish (not a whale), brought back from running away from his mission. Jonah did not want to be "a light to lighten the gentiles,"[12] but, as a man of God, inevitably he was.

Isaiah's seed was germinating. Actually, it had gone about as far as so open an idea was going to go before Jesus of Nazareth burst on the scene. This was the climax of the great plot of the Old Testament. Unintentional as the drama may originally have been, it issued in the world's most dramatic event: the coming of Christ.

Human nature being what it is, the concept of everybody loving everybody just does not flower easily. "Who is my neighbor?"[13] is a question deeply rooted in the human psyche. The breaking of the "I against you" complex is a tremendously difficult process. An even more difficult one, apparently, is the breaking of the "we against them" complex. Just how difficult is clearly indicated by the disciples of Jesus himself. Their final question, incredibly, put to the Master immediately before his ascension into Heaven, was, "Lord, will you at this time restore the kingdom to Israel?"[14] The most inappropriate farewell in history!

For many months the disciples had heard nothing but Jesus' gracious gospel of love, and yet here they were still thinking in terms of Israel. Indeed, it would be my thought that this is why Judas betrayed his Master. He himself felt betrayed. Jesus had not overthrown the Romans.

To this day the world is saddled with the "we vs. them" syndrome, and so it will be, I suppose, as long as human beings continue to be human. "We vs. them" is really only a more sophisticated form of "I vs. you." One simply withdraws into the security of the group: be it "the gang" at the school, the clique at the club or the flag-wavers at the capitol. Even churches are not immune to this syndrome. How stedfastly some denominations resist any steps towards unity with churches of a slightly different point of view! For ancient Israel, the church and the nation were the same thing. Thus, as we shall see, the Israelites were doubly locked into "we vs. them." This, in turn, led them to interpret the dreadful events which befell them as evidences of a wrathful, punitive God. Why else would his chosen people so suffer?

It took the entire 1500 years of Old Testament history to bring the Hebrew people even close to recognizing that their sufferings were not unique and that God was not necessarily the immediate source of them. Be it noted here, however, that these people were, as far as a sense of responsibility is concerned, far ahead of anyone else.

In the Old Testament we trace not the education of God, as in "The Green Pastures," but the education of a people - education to the stage wherein the concept of a universal God, a God of love and forebearance, rather than one of partiality, anger and vengeance, could be grasped, if barely.

The preacher and exemplar of such a religion in its purity was derided and crucified. The New Testament gives four accounts of his life, teachings, death, resurrection and ascension. They differ about as much as one would expect them to under the circumstances. (We will deal with this in chapters following.) But the accounts are incredibly beautiful and deeply moving.

The New Testament also tells how enough people (all Jews, by the way) did take hold of Jesus' message, went forth and initiated a process which continues to this day. This, of course, is the process of spreading the news, the crucial news that God loves the world, and loves all of it. Added to this is the equally crucial assurance that he gives us his own Spirit to enable us to do likewise.

Is the Bible true? The answer is yes. It is terribly true, revealing as it does, openly and without comment, the thoughts and actions of a people who were human to the nth degree, but who one way or another got hold of one overriding idea - the idea that God is one and righteous. It is obvious that God thus got hold of them, and in the course of fifteen centuries brought their thinking along. Thus in the later years, the prophet Micah could write "...and what does the Lord require of you but to do justice, to love kindness, and to walk humbly with your God?"[15] This is one solid way in which divine inspiration took place: in a great idea which grew up. And this was ultimately rewarded by as total a revelation of the Divine Nature as can be made without trespassing on human freedom. At least this is what all Christians believe of Jesus of Nazareth. His majestic story we find in the New Testament.

This, then, is the Bible; a thoroughly human book, but a book which is nevertheless divine. This also is what makes of the Bible something of an enigma. As in life, so in books, divinity must shine through humanity. God's truth does not come gift-wrapped. When reading the Bible, we must not forget this. If we do, we are headed either for a massive task of self-deception or for a massive dose of disillusionment. Remembering the human element, however, we are utterly amazed at what divine inspiration actually can do.

NOTES

1. Joshua 6ff.
2. Matthew 5:44
3. II Kings 1:1-9
4. Luke 9:55
5. Genesis 4:1-16
6. Genesis 6-8
7. Genesis 18, 19
8. Exodus 20:1-17, Deuteronomy 5:6-21
9. Leviticus
10. Isaiah 55:5
11. Jonah 4:11
12. Luke 2:32a (KJV)
13. Luke 10:29b
14. Acts 1:6b
15. Micah 6:8b

IV

DIVINE INSPIRATION

IT IS NOT ENOUGH to trace the effects of the divine influence on the thinking of the patriarchs and prophets of a God-conscious people - effects which showed themselves over a long period of time. Divine inspiration works in a myriad of ways, of some of which we are undoubtedly unaware. But there are instances when its influence is so apparent that to deny it would be like denying the brilliance of the full moon.

It is the Christian conviction that St. Paul was correct when he told the Athenians that God "is not far from each one of us,"[1] and that this is the way that it always has been and always will be. As we have stated before, this shows in everyone's life to a greater or lesser degree. But there are those in whose deeds and words it shows beyond all doubt. The point before us here is that the Old Testament, with all of its disturbing characteristics and unacceptable attitudes, nevertheless contains an amazing number of passages which cannot be explained as anything other than the results of divine promptings. At one point here and another there, Old Testament seers - pilgrims who "did not receive what was promised"[2] - still touched home, "having seen it and greeted it from afar,"[3] and their visions and greetings stand out in the book, as do brilliant stars and planets against the lesser luminaries of the night.

In the New Testament this phenomenon becomes so apparent that it is as if the sun had risen and had cast its rays from one end of the work to the other. We are dealing there with words and deeds so transparently inspired that the effect is overwhelming. The only way to avoid this effect is not to read the book. We will come to this in due course, but here our considerations will dwell on a few of those passages in the "Old Book" - passages which reveal what can actually happen in the human heart, and which, to my mind at least, prove Paul's Athenian contention that God is always close at hand. Ultimately it is exactly this which makes possible the longer process of revelation referred to above.

There is, for instance, Jacob's dream, rightly famous - the dream which he had while fleeing from his brother's wrath. In a foreign country, a country which he assumed was under the aegis of a foreign god, Jacob saw a ladder:

> *...a ladder set up on the earth, and the top of it reached to heaven; and behold, the angels of God were ascending and descending on it! And behold, the Lord stood above it and said, "I am the Lord, the God of Abraham your father and the God of Isaac..."*[4]

Thus Jacob learned of the universality of God. His reaction, naturally enough, was unworthy of the vision: he bargained with the Lord. We just do not grow up all at once. The remarkable feature of the story, however, lies in the fact that, in the course of time, Jacob did grow in spite of himself. He was indeed an archetype of his people, who, as we have already observed, also grew in spite of themselves.

It was some twenty years later that Jacob, having worn out his welcome in Haran, found it necessary to return to Canaan. This, of course, meant at last facing his offended brother, Esau. More than that, it meant facing himself: a scheming fellow who had deceived his father, robbed his brother and cheated his uncle. The story of his wrestling with the angel at the stream, Jabbok,[5] is full of primitive ideas and strange preconceptions. (Angels cannot abide daylight, names carry magic powers, food-taboos derive from the encounter.) But the message of the conflict is loud and clear - and worthy: God opposes our selfish ways, and when we strive for his blessing, he changes us. That Jacob became a changed man is borne out by the rest of his story. This, of course, is the forerunner of the story of Israel, and, appropriately, it was to Israel that the angel changed Jacob's name.

Another account among many in which we cannot but feel the divine pulse is the one detailing David's retreat before the rebel forces of his self-seeking son, Absalom. A more ignominious situation for a king would be hard to imagine. But that was not all. As he rode down the hot, dusty road to Bahurim,

> *...there came out one of the family of the house of Saul, whose name was Shimei, the son of Gera; and as he came he cursed continually. And he threw stones at David, and at all the servants of King David...Then Abishai the son of Zeruiah said to the King, "Why should this dead dog curse my Lord the King? Let me go over and take off his head." But the King said, "What have I to do with you, you sons of Zeruiah? If he is cursing because the Lord has said to him, 'Curse David,' who then shall say, 'Why have you done so?'...Behold my own son seeks my life; how much more now may this Benjaminite!"*[6]

Shimei continued to throw stones and fling dust, but David, in spite of all of his sins (or perhaps because of them), continued to exercise that restraint which was later exemplified by that one "who when he was reviled, he did not revile in return."[7]

The Old Testament is replete with stories illustrative of noble attitudes in the midst of elemental reactions, great spirit in the context of primitive ideas: such accounts as those of Abraham and the three angels,[8] the (almost) sacrifice of Isaac,[9] the history of Joseph,[10] Moses and the burning bush,[11] Balaam and Balak,[12] Ruth,[13] Elisha, Naaman and Gehazi[14] - the list goes on and on.

The Book is also filled with unforgettable "one-liners," beginning with Cain's self-incriminating remark, "Am I my brother's keeper?"[15] We find them everywhere: "But Lot's wife... looked back and... became a pillar of salt."[16] There is Elijah's memorable "still small voice,"[17] Elisha's "fear not, for those who are with us are more than those who are with them,"[18] and Solomon's "But will God indeed dwell on the earth? Behold heaven and the highest heaven cannot contain thee, how much less this house which I have built?"[19]

Where should we end? Job gave us "Naked I came from my mother's womb, and naked shall I return; the Lord gave and the Lord has taken away; blessed be the name of the Lord."[20] It was Jeremiah who asked whether the leopard could change his spots,[21] Daniel who contributed the "feet of clay"[22] and the "handwriting on the wall"[23] and Hoseah who said, "for they sow the wind, and they shall reap the whirlwind."[24] To Habakkuk we owe "so he may run who reads it" and that incomparable line, "But the Lord is in his holy temple; let all the earth keep silence before him."[25] Indeed, the third chapter of Habakkuk, whether it be read as imagery (for a foreign invasion) or as the interpretation of some natural cataclysm, is one of gripping grandeur. We cannot read the Old Testament without recognizing that a large portion of it is great literature, and that the reason for this is simply that it expresses great thoughts. This, I hold, has its origin in a higher realm.

We need not present here a complete review of the Psalms, any more than of the many prophets, but it does fall to this work to point out that amidst much dross and more "we vs. them" hatred (both characteristic of the historical portions also), we find passages which nevertheless sweep us off our feet. In that extraordinary collection of poems known as the Psalms we find:

> *Blessed is the man that hath not walked in the counsel of the ungodly, nor stood in the way of sinners, and hath not sat in the seat of the scornful.*[26]
>
> ---
>
> *O Lord our Governor, how excellent is thy name in all the world, thou that hast set thy glory above the heavens!*
>
> *Out of the mouths of very babes and sucklings hast thou ordained strength, because of thine enemies, that thou mightest still the enemy and the avenger. When I consider the heavens even the work of thy fingers; the moon and the stars which thou hast ordained;*
>
> *What is man, that thou art mindful of him? And the son of man, that thou visitest him?*[27]
>
> ---
>
> *The Lord is my shepherd...*[28]
>
> ---

The earth is the Lord's and all that therein is...[29]

The Lord is my light and my salvation; whom then shall I fear? The Lord is the strength of my life; of whom then shall I be afraid?[30]

I will lift up mine eyes unto the hills; from whence cometh my help? My help cometh even from the Lord, who hath made heaven and earth.[31]

Out of the deep have I called unto thee, O Lord; Lord, hear my voice. O let thine ears consider well the voice of my complaint.

If thou, Lord, wilt be extreme to mark what is done amiss, O Lord, who may abide it?

For there is mercy with thee; therefore shalt thou be feared.

I look for the Lord; my soul doth wait for him; in his word is my trust.

My soul fleeth unto the Lord before the morning watch; I say, before the morning watch.

O Israel, trust in the Lord; for with the Lord there is mercy, and with him is plenteous redemption.

And he shall redeem Israel from all his sins.[32]

O Lord, thou hast searched me out and known me. Thou knowest my down-sitting, and mine up-rising; thou understandeth my thoughts long before.

Thou art about my path, and about my bed, and art acquainted with all my ways.[33]

Let everything that hath breath praise the Lord.[34]

Yes, there are imprecations against adversaries, rather savage ones too, and many evidences of less than universal objectives. We hardly approve, for instance, of the sentiments found in: "These also that seek the hurt of my soul, they shall go under the earth. Let them fall upon the edge of the sword, that they may be a portion for foxes."[35] Nor do we rise to: "The Lord hath said, I will bring my people again, as I did from Bashan; mine own will I bring again, as I did sometime from the deep of the sea. That thy foot may be dipped in the blood of thine enemies, and that the tongue of thy dogs may be red through the same."[36] Our hearts stand still when English choir boys are faced with these words at Evensong. But the point here is that God does break through all this time and again so that the psalmists could sing:

> *Be still then, and know that I am God: I will be exalted among the nations, and I will be exalted in the earth.*[37]

> *For all the world shall worship thee, sing of thee, and praise thy Name.*[38]

> *God be merciful unto us, and bless us, and show us the light of his countenance, and be merciful unto us;*
>
> *That thy way may be known upon earth, thy saving health among all nations.*[39]

> *The Lord is nigh unto all them that call upon him; yea, all such as call upon him faithfully.*[40]

And finally,

> *All nations whom thou hast made shall come and worship thee, O Lord; and shall glorify thy name.*[41]

It should be noted here that the Psalms, for all of their sometime reflection of a less than universal attitude, are nevertheless so overwhelmingly personal and deeply introspective that, in spite of themselves, they speak a universal language. It is no accident that people of many faiths, and often of little faith, find in them a source of enormous encouragement and intense inner strength. The Psalms celebrate the reality of an ever-present higher power. People everywhere identify with this. Such is divine inspiration in full bloom.

NOTES

1. Acts 17:27b
2. Hebrews 11:39b
3. Hebrews 11:13b
4. Genesis 28:12b-13a
5. Genesis 32:22-32
6. 2 Samuel 16:5-14
7. 1 Peter 2:23
8. Genesis 18
9. Genesis22
10. Genesis 37-50
11. Exodus 3
12. Numbers 22-24
13. The Book of Ruth
14. 2 Kings 5
15. Genesis 4:9b
16. Genesis 19:26
17. 1 Kings 19:12
18. 2 Kings 6:16
19. 1 Kings 8:27
20. Job 1:21
21. Jeremiah 13:23
22. Daniel 2:25-49
23. Daniel 5
24. Hosea 8:7
25. Habakkuk 2:2b, 2:30
26. Psalm 1:1

27. Psalm 8:1-4
28. Psalm 23:1a
29. Psalm 24:1a
30. Psalm 27:1
31. Psalm 121:1
32. Psalm 130
33. Psalm 139:1, 2
34. Psalm 150:6
35. Psalm 63:10, 11
36. Psalm 68:22, 23
37. Psalm 46:10
38. Psalm 66:3
39. Psalm 67:1, 2
40. Psalm 145:18
41. Psalm 86:9

V

THE PROPHETS

TURNING TO THE PROPHETS, we are confronted with a vast array of literature, much of it burning with indignation against the people of Israel for their many sins. One gets the distinct impression that the other nations are mere arrows in the Lord's quiver, to be shot at Israel when it serves the Lord's purpose. Further, we are not a little disturbed by a God so wrathful that he almost seems to delight in strewing the streets with bodies and the fields with blood. Ezekiel tells us of divine executioners being sent against the apostates in Jerusalem with instructions to "pass through the city..., and smite; your eye shall not spare, and you shall show no pity; slay old men outright, young men and maidens, little children and women..."[1] On the other hand, against the enemies of his people, the Lord prompts Ezekiel to prophesy, "And I will fill your mountains with the slain; on your hills and in your valleys and in all your ravines those slain with the sword shall fall. I will make you a perpetual desolation, and your cities shall not be inhabited. Then you will know that I am the Lord."[2]

One hardly gets the feeling that we are dealing with the God of Jesus - Jesus, who taught us to love our enemies and to forgive seventy times seven times. Alas, Ezekiel is not the only prophet who speaks in these unforgiving terms. Death and destruction are thought of as God's principal instruments. They are to be visited upon Israel for her sins and then upon her enemies for administering them. Those hapless adversaries, after duly punishing Israel, are in their turn, to be duly punished. Nobody wins! We are back to the God of the flood: certainly not a very nice Deity. And we find traces of this sort of thinking in virtually all of the prophets. As we do today, so they lived in a strife-torn, violent world. Like us, they had their own difficulties interpreting the times. Unlike us, they did not know of the man from Nazareth.

All of this notwithstanding, the compassionate Lord clearly breaks through in a number of the prophets' writings, and those break-throughs issue in some of the world's most moving passages. "We vs. them" actually shows signs of wear. A new ideal begins to emerge.

Isaiah, a book with perhaps as many as three different authors, is a veritable symphony of majestic chords. Yes, there are some discordant ones too, in which the Lord is "enraged against all the nations,"[3] but the dominant theme is superb:

> *It shall come to pass in the latter days that the mountain of the house of the Lord shall be established as the highest of the mountains, and shall be raised above the hills; and all the nations shall flow into it, and many peoples shall come, and say, "Come, let us go up to the mountain of the Lord, to the house of the God of Jacob; that he may teach us his ways and that we may walk in his paths." For out of Zion shall go forth the law, and the word of the Lord from Jerusalem. He shall judge between the nations, and they shall beat their swords into plowshares , and their spears into pruning hooks; nation shall not lift up sword against nation, neither shall they learn war any-more.*[4]

Placed thus on the podium, the children of Israel were nevertheless a long way from being in tune with such music, and Isaiah's consequent mission was too awesome even for such a prophet. But who can count out the Deity? And so we read:

In the year that King Uzziah died I saw the Lord sitting upon a throne, high and lifted up; and his train filled the temple. Above him stood the seraphim; each had six wings: with two he covered his face, with two he covered his feet, and with two he flew. And one called to another and said: "Holy, holy, holy, is the Lord of hosts; the whole earth is full of his glory." And the foundation of the thresholds shook at the voice of him who called, and the house was filled with smoke. And I said: "Woe is me! For I am lost; for I am a man of unclean lips, and I dwell in the midst of a people of unclean lips; for my eyes have seen the King, the Lord of hosts!"

Then flew one of the seraphim to me, having in his hand a burning coal which he had taken with tongs from the altar. And he touched my mouth, and said: "Behold this has touched your lips; your guilt is taken away, and your sin forgiven." And I heard the voice of the Lord saying, "Whom shall I send, and who will go for us?" Then I said, "Here I am! Send me !"[5]

This, of course, reveals the ultimate source of the strength of such prophets as those involved in that extraordinary series of books. Thus we read further on in Isaiah:

Have you not known? Have you not heard? The Lord is the everlasting God, the Creator of the ends of the earth. He does not faint or grow weary, his understanding is unsearchable. He gives power to the faint, and to him who has no might he increases strength. Even youths shall faint and be weary, and young men shall fall exhausted;

> *but they who wait for the Lord shall renew their strength, they shall mount up with wings like eagles, they shall run and not be weary, they shall walk and not faint.*[6]

This being the case, all people in all places at all times can give ear to no loftier call than that made in a subsequent chapter:

> *Seek the Lord while he may be found, call upon him while he is near, let the wicked forsake his way, and the unrighteous man his thoughts; let him return to the Lord, that he may have mercy on him; and to our God, for he will abundantly pardon.*[7]

As we have seen in the Psalms, this theme of divine forgiveness appears several times in the "Old Book", but in no place more vividly than in the prophet Joel:

> *Blow the trumpet in Zion; sound the alarm on my holy mountain! Let all the inhabitants of the land tremble, for the day of the Lord is coming, it is near..."Yet even now," says the Lord, "return to me with all your heart, with fasting, with weeping, and with mourning; and rend yours hearts and not your garments." Return to the Lord your God, for he is gracious and merciful, slow to anger, and abiding in stedfast love, and repents of evil.*[8]

That the Divine is speaking through the prophet, Amos, is hard to deny when we read:

> *I hate, I despise your feasts, and I take no delight in your solemn assemblies. Even though you offer me your burnt offerings and your cereal offerings, I will not accept them, and the peace offerings of your fatted beasts I will not look upon. Take away from me the noise of your songs; to the melody of your harps I will not listen. But let*

> *justice roll down like waters, and righteousness like an ever-flowing stream.*[9]

For many of us, the mysterious prophet, Habakkuk, has the last word:

> *Though the fig tree do not blossom, nor fruit be on the vines, the produce of the olive fail and fields yield no food, the flock be cut off from the fold and there be no herd in the stalls, yet I will rejoice in the Lord, I will joy in the God of my salvation.*[10]

The point of all this being that God in his mercy touches every person in every age. Sometimes he breaks through, "for thou, Lord, hast never failed them that seek thee."[11] It is to the everlasting credit of the ancient Hebrews that with all of their transgressions and clannish ferocity, they were nevertheless a peculiarly "turned on" people. There seems always to have been someone among them who was especially "turned on," and who fearlessly championed the living God. To all of these the living God gave the power and the glory of his presence, so that succeeding generations around the globe have given to their writings the label, "holy." What other people can claim this?

It is difficult indeed to deny divine inspiration in passages such as the few samples quoted. Here were relatively elemental people speaking out in relatively elemental times. What they expressed had very little to do with human nature as we know it. Moreover, like the Israelis of today, they lived under tremendous pressures exerted by enemies on every side. But difficulties which can bring out the worst in some people can also bring out the best in others. Thus the words of the Jewish prophets come ringing down through the ages, and the ages listen in awe. It was not a case of great poets giving us a splendid God. It was, rather, a case of a splendid God giving us great poets.

NOTES

1. Ezekiel 9:5b, 6a
2. Ezekiel 35:8, 9
3. Isaiah 34:2a
4. Isaiah 2:2-4
5. Isaiah 6:1-8
6. Isaiah 40: 28-31
7. Isaiah 55: 6-7
8. Joel 2: 1, 12, 13
9. Amos 5: 21-24
10. Habakkuk 3: 17, 18
11. Psalm 9: 10b

VI

THE PROPHECIES

There are in the Old Testament certain portions which go beyond those passionate passages having to do with human behavior and its connection with the divine. We have in the "Old Book" a number of mysterious verses, some of which can be partially explained as applying to Israel as a nation, and some to then contemporary events or individuals, but all of which, in view of subsequent happenings, defy the sort of explanation usually considered as final. To many people they can be comprehended only in the light of the unity of history: a history which to them, at least, is seen as always under the influence of one and the same God, "in [whom] we live and move and have our being."[1]

There is, for instance, that puzzling incident in the story of Abraham in which Melchizedec, then King of Salem (later Jerusalem), not a Hebrew, came out to meet him bringing bread and wine:

> *...he was priest of God Most High. And he blessed him and said, "Blessed be Abraham by God Most High, maker of heaven and earth; and blessed be God Most High, who has delivered your enemies into your hand!" And Abraham gave him a tenth of everything.*[2]

This, of course, was the passage seized upon by another mysterious writer, the author of the Epistle to the Hebrews, who, centuries later, wrote:

> *We have this as a rare and steadfast anchor of the soul, a hope that enters into the inner shrine behind the curtain, where Jesus has gone as a forerunner on our behalf, having become a high priest for ever after the order of Melchizedek."*[3]

So Melchizedek comes out of Jerusalem when it was still the Canaanite city of Salem, bearing bread and wine, not to reemerge in the "Old Book", except in an extraordinarily prophetic reference in the Psalms:

> *In the day of thy power shall thy people offer themselves willingly with an holy worship: thy young men shall come to thee as dew from the womb of the morning.*
>
> *The Lord sware, and will not repent, Thou art a Priest for ever after the order of Melchizedek.*[4]

From the New Testament point of view, Melchizedek is the prototype of the Host at the Last Supper. But the fact that he is there at all - in Genesis - continues to amaze us.

St. Luke tells us that Jesus, on his famous walk to Emmaus, after his resurrection, interpreted to the two awe-struck disciples "in all the scriptures the things concerning himself."[5] How we would like to know what "the things" were! Luke says that he began with Moses. In his "Book of the Acts of the Apostles" Luke goes on to tell how Peter quoted Moses from Deuteronomy:

> *The Lord your God will raise up for you a prophet like me from among you, from your brethren - him you shall heed...*[6]

Perhaps this was Jesus' number one. Peter also quotes Psalm 16:

> *I have set the Lord always before me; for he is on my right hand...*
>
> *For why? thou shalt not leave my soul in hell; neither shalt thou suffer thy Holy One to see corruption.*[7]

And Psalm 110 (again!):

The Lord said unto my Lord, Sit thou on my right hand, until I make thine enemies thy footstool.[8]

In this latter quote Peter had earlier authority from Jesus himself, who used it to confute the scribes.[9]

If we cannot cite all of the passages which Jesus quoted to his disciples as those "concerning himself," certainly we can note a few which appear obvious.

In Isaiah, a book which is a veritable treasure-trove of heavenly wisdom and wonder, we read:

The people who walked in darkness have seen a great light; those who dwelt in a land of deep darkness, on them has light shined. Thou hast multiplied the nation, thou hast increased its joy; they rejoice before thee as with joy at the harvest, as men rejoice when they divide the spoil. For the yoke of his burden and the staff for his shoulder, the rod of his oppressor, thou hast broken as on the day of Midian. For every boot of the tramping warrior in battle tumult and every garment rolled in blood will be burned as fuel for the fire.

For to us a child is born, to us a son is given; and the government will be upon his shoulder, and his name will be called "Wonderful Counselor, Mighty God, Everlasting Father, Prince of Peace." Of the increase of his government and of peace there will be no end, upon the throne of David, and over his kingdom, to establish it and to uphold it with justice and with righteousness from this time forth and forevermore. The zeal of the Lord of hosts will do this.[10]

Couple this amazing passage with one some chapters later, and we readily understand why Christians have read them avidly Christmas after Christmas:

> *Comfort, comfort, my people, says your God. Speak tenderly to Jerusalem, and cry to her that her warfare is ended, that her iniquity is pardoned, that she has received from the Lord's hand double for all her sins.*
>
> *A voice cries: "In the wilderness prepare the way of the Lord, make straight in the desert a highway for our God. Every valley shall be made low; the uneven ground shall become level, and the rough places a plain. And the glory of the Lord shall be revealed, and all flesh shall see it together, for the mouth of the Lord has spoken ...*
>
> *Get you up to a high mountain, O Zion, herald of good tidings; lift up your voice with strength, O Jerusalem, herald of good tidings, lift it up, fear not; say to the cities of Judah, "Behold your God!" Behold, the Lord God comes with might, and his arm rules for him; behold, his reward is with him, and his recompense before him. He will feed his flock like a shepherd, he will gather the lambs in his arms, he will carry them in his bosom, and gently lead those that are with young.*[11]

Regardless of the original intent of this passage, whatever it might have been, how can one possibly avoid connecting these words with what happened in Jerusalem seven centuries later?

Then there is that strange passage in Micah:

> *But you, O Bethlehem Ephratha, who are little to be among the clans of Judah, from you shall come forth for me one who is to be ruler in Israel, whose origin is from old, from ancient days. Therefore he shall give them up until the time when she who is in travail has brought forth; then the rest of his brethren shall return to the people of Israel. And he shall stand and feed his flock in the strength of the Lord, in the majesty of the name of the Lord his God. And they shall dwell secure, for now he shall be great to the ends of the earth.*[12]

One must be quick to add that the author of this famous passage probably had in mind no such event as the coming of Jesus Christ, but rather the return of exiles to Jerusalem. Further, he was very much of a "we vs. them" point of view. But there the passage is. Subsequent occurrences have brought it to the fore, and no amount of scholarly analysis can push it back into the shades of controversy. Unless the nativity passages in Matthew and Luke are in error, the prophecy simply came true.

More to the point is another passage from Isaiah which Jesus himself chose to use as prophetic of his ministry:

> *The Spirit of the Lord God is upon me, because the Lord has anointed me to bring good tidings to the afflicted; he has sent me to bind up the brokenhearted, to proclaim liberty to the captives, and the opening of the prison to those who are bound; to proclaim the year of the Lord's favor, and the day of vengeance of our God; to comfort all who mourn ...*[13]

Indeed, it is extremely interesting to note how Jesus edited this passage, which he was at liberty to do, given the biblical transcriptions at hand: "the opening of the prison to those who are bound" becomes the "recovering of sight to the blind," and "day of vengeance of our God" becomes "the acceptable year of the Lord."[14]

For yet another passage we need no further testimony as to its ultimate fulfillment, intended or unintended, than that of the Master. This one is from Zechariah:

> *Rejoice greatly, O daughter of Zion! Shout aloud, O daughter of Jerusalem! Lo, your king comes to you; triumphant and victorious is he, humble and riding on an ass, on a colt, the foal of an ass. I will cut off the chariot from Ephraim and the war horse from Jerusalem; and the battle bow shall be cut off, and he shall command peace to the nations; his kingdom shall be from sea to sea, and from the River to the ends of the earth.*[15]

In acting out this prophecy on what is now thought of as the first "Palm Sunday," Jesus was publicly proclaiming his messiahship. More than that, he was testifying to the sort of messiah that he was: humble, a man of peace. Definitely he was not the one to lead Israel against her enemies. But this second part of the proclamation did not sink in, at least not at first. Even on that unforgettable walk to Emmaus, after Jesus' resurrection, Cleopas and the other disciple declared that they thought that "he was the one to redeem Israel."[16] But Zechariah had spoken of "peace to the nations" - not simply to Israel.

We come now to the most moving of "the prophecies." With these it is still more difficult to explain the passages involved as referring only to Israel, if at all.

We turn back to that Old Testament book of books, Isaiah, and we find:

> *Behold, my servant shall prosper, he shall be exalted and lifted up, and shall be very high.*

We read on, and are stunned:

> *As many were astonished at him - his appearance was so marred, beyond human semblance, and his form beyond that of the sons of men - so shall he startle many nations; kings shall shut their mouths because of him; for that which has not been told them they shall see, and that which they have not heard they shall understand.*
>
> *Who has believed what we have heard? And to whom has the arm of the Lord been revealed? For he grew up before him like a young plant, and like a root out of dry ground, he had no form or comeliness that we should look at him.*
>
> *He was despised and rejected by men; a man of sorrows, and acquainted with grief; and as one from whom men hide their faces he was despised, and we esteemed him not.*[17]

Here the music of Handel takes over, a fitting accompaniment to one of the world's most magnificent passages:

> *Surely he has borne our griefs and carried our sorrows; yet we esteemed him stricken, smitten by God, and afflicted. But he was wounded for our transgressions, he was bruised for our iniquities; upon him was the chastisement that made us whole, and with his stripes we are healed.*

All we like sheep have gone astray, we have turned every one to his own way; and the Lord has laid on him the iniquity of us all.[18]

It seems impossible that more could be said, or that the Gospel, as we know it, could be given a more telling preview. And the seer writes on:

He was oppressed, and he was afflicted, yet he opened not his mouth. By oppression and judgment he was taken away; and as for his generation, who considered that he was cut off out of the land of the living, stricken for the transgressions of my people?

And they made his grave with the wicked and with a rich man in his death, although he had done no violence, and there was no deceit in his mouth.[19]

It is difficult to continue to read these astounding words without thinking of "de Lawd" of "The Green Pastures": the sad personage leaning on his roll-top desk, his eyes cast down, while his Son, apparently forsaken, endures the cross. And so we find it in Isaiah:

Yet it was the will of the Lord to bruise him; he has put him to grief, when he makes himself an offering for sin, he shall see his offspring, he shall prolong his days; the will of the Lord shall prosper in his hand; he shall see the fruit of the travail of his soul and be satisfied; by his knowledge shall the righteous one, my servant, make many to be accounted righteous; and he shall bear their iniquities.

Therefore I shall divide him a portion of the great, and he shall divide the spoil with the strong; because he poured out his soul to death, and was numbered with the transgressors; yet he bore the sin of many, and made intercession for the transgressors.[20]

What else can we see in this astonishing scripture than the happenings on Calvary seven hundred years later: not only the happenings but also their effects? And what else can we say but that the writer was plumbing the depths, and that in this case he clearly saw what God would ultimately have to do? This was precisely what would be required in order to reach not only Israel but also the whole round world.

NOTES

1. Acts 17: 28 a
2. Genesis 14: 18-20
3. Hebrews 6: 19, 20
4. Psalm 110: 3, 4
5. Luke 24: 27 b
6. Deuteronomy 18: 15
7. Psalm 16: 9 a, 11
8. Psalm 110: 1
9. Mark 12: 36
10. Isaiah 9:2-7
11. Isaiah 40:1-5, 9-11
12. Micah 5:2-4
13. Isaiah 61:1,2
14. Luke 4:18,19
15. Zechariah 9:9-10
16. Luke 24:21
17. Isaiah 52:13-53:3
18. Isaiah 53:4-6
19. Isaiah 53:7-9
20. Isaiah 53:10-12

VII

THE ULTIMATE MARK

THOSE OF US who live on this side of the coming of Jesus of Nazareth can have little or no idea of what it must have been like to live on the other. Imagine the perplexity as to the evil in the world, and the agony over the question of the attitude of the Creator, if indeed there even were one. It was, perhaps, out of such a quandary that an unknown psalmist, tenacious in his conviction as to God's invisible presence, but surrounded by the scornful, wrote what now appears as nothing less than a miraculous poem:

> *My God, my God, look upon me; why hast thou forsaken me? and art so far from my health, and from the words of my complaint?*
>
> *O my God, I cry in the day-time, but thou hearest not; and in the night season also I take no rest.*
>
> *And thou continuest holy, O thou worship of Israel.*
>
> *Our fathers hoped in thee; they trusted in thee, and thou didst deliver them.*
>
> *They called upon thee and were holpen; they put their trust in thee, and were not confounded.*
>
> *But as for me, I am a worm, and no man; a very scorn of men, and the outcast of the people.*

All they that see me laugh me to scorn; they shoot out their lips, and shake their heads, saying,

He trusted in the Lord, that he would deliver him; let him deliver him, if he will have him.

But thou art he who took me out of my mother's womb; thou wast my hope, when I hanged yet upon my mother's breasts.

I have been left unto thee since I was born; thou art my God even from my mother's womb.

O go not from me; for trouble is hard at hand, and there is none to help me.

Many oxen are come about me; fat bulls of Bashan close me in on every side.

They gape upon me with their mouths, as it were a ramping and a roaring lion.

I am poured out like water, and all my bones are out of joint; my heart also in the midst of my body is even like melting wax.

My strength is dried up like a potsherd, and my tongue cleaveth to my gums, and thou bringest me into the dust of death.

For many dogs are come about me, and the council of the wicked layeth siege against me.

They pierced my hands and my feet: I may tell all my bones: they stand staring and looking upon me.

They part my garments among them, and cast lots upon my vesture.

But be not thou far from me, O Lord; thou art my succour, haste thee to help me.[1]

All of which brings forth the inevitable question: Did the Gospel writers make the passion of Jesus fit this psalm, or did the psalm accurately predict the passion? We will never know (this side of Jordan), but the solid testimony of all four Gospels, so prone to disagree on small points, varies on but few of the details set forth in the psalm. Only John notes that one item, the casting of lots for the garments, fulfills this psalm.[2] The others, obviously, were simply writing their versions of what happened.

The cry of despair with which the psalm begins, but which is so ameliorated by the later verses, is recorded by both Mark and Matthew as the final cry of Jesus -with no reference to the psalm whatsoever. Indeed, it seems evident that this detail is one of the marks of authenticity in those two Gospels. We have already noted Mark's basic belief in Jesus' divinity. Here we note that he did not turn aside from recording what might be considered as contradictory evidence, which, we should also note, both Luke and John did. Both of the latter failed to record the cry. It was, apparently, an embarrassment to them.

To my mind, at least, the psalm remains one of those extraordinary prophecies: mysterious they are, and often inexplicable. Of other prophecies we take note of just two more.

Peter quoted one of these to the crowd in Jerusalem on the day of Pentecost (after Jesus' resurrection), citing its fulfillment in the ecstatic utterances of the disciples. It comes from the fifth century (B.C.) prophet, Joel:

> *And it shall come to pass afterwards, that I will pour out my spirit on all flesh; your sons and your daughters shall prophesy, your old men shall dream dreams, and your young men shall see visions. Even upon the menservants and maidservants in those days, I will pour out my spirit. And I will give portents in the heavens and on the earth, blood and fire and columns of smoke. The sun shall be turned to darkness, and the moon to blood, before the great and terrible day of the Lord comes. And it shall come to pass that all who call upon the name of the Lord shall be delivered ...*[3]

Here again the fulfillment of this prophecy went far beyond the vision of the prophet. Joel had as insular a point of view as any of his colleagues, but the passage leapt into Peter's mind, as it undoubtedly did into the minds of his Jewish audience.

Parenthetically, one should note here that the prophet's references to "blood, fire and columns of smoke," to the sun being turned to darkness and the moon to blood - these references, which are used by others of the prophets[4] and, indeed, by Jesus himself,[5] did not faze Peter in connection with the event at hand. We should remember this whenever we deal with such passages in Scripture. Biblical people spoke in biblical terms, which almost inevitably were highly poetic. Such colorful imagery was seldom intended as anything but exactly that: imagery. Our western literalism often serves us ill when we read these imaginative passages.

Of the many passages in the Old Testament which might be considered as prophetic of the New, and were so used by the Apostles, perhaps the most obvious one is Jeremiah's outright prediction of a new covenant:

> *Behold, the days are coming, says the Lord, when I will make a new covenant with the house of Israel and the house of Judah, not like the covenant which I made with their fathers when I took them by the hand to bring them out of the land of Egypt, my covenant which they broke, though I was their husband, says the Lord. But this is the covenant which I will make with the house of Israel after those days, says the Lord: I will put my law within them, and I will write it upon their hearts; and I will be their God, and they shall be my people. And no longer shall each man teach his neighbor and each his brother, saying, "Know the Lord," for they shall all know me, from the least of them to the greatest, says the Lord; for I will forgive their iniquity, and I will remember their sin no more.*[6]

It was this passage which Jesus undoubtedly had in mind when he spoke of the new covenant at the last supper.[7] Paul refers to it in Romans and in Second Corinthians,[8] and the writer of Hebrews quotes it in full.[9] However, *all* of these writers lifted it out of the context of "the house of Israel and the house of Judah." And this, of course, is the great dividing line between the Old Testament and the New. It is the ultimate mark, I believe, at which the entire Old Testament is aimed: the concept of a universal God.

From the Christian point of view, it is an amazing fact that the Messiah, so long awaited by this gifted people - the Hebrews, did not come until the western world had taken on a pluralistic cast under the unity forced upon it by the Roman Empire. Further, when he did come, he did not come simply to deliver those people. As we have observed, the most profound of their prophets had actually foreseen - as through a glass darkly - that the Messiah when he came would hardly be small:

> *Wonderful Counselor, Mighty God, Everlasting Father, Prince of Peace.*[10]

> *... he shall command peace to the nations; his dominion shall be from sea to sea, and from the River to the ends of the earth.*[11]

The Jews of today are still waiting for that Messiah. In view of the New Testament, so overwhelming in its majesty, one wonders what they are waiting for. The irony of it all is that Christianity, the religion emanating from the New Testament (however laboriously) is a thoroughly Jewish religion. The whole concept of a messiah is Jewish to begin with, and the entire Old Testament leads to Jesus' principles to end with.

Without the Hebrew people, their history and their literature, Jesus' mission to the world could hardly have been accomplished. "For salvation," John quotes Jesus as saying, "is from the Jews."[12] Paul, in his missionary endeavors, was almost totally dependent on his hearers' Jewish background. Even the Greeks and Romans who were persuaded by him had, in most instances, some familiarity - either by marriage or other close association - with the Jewish mind. The first thing which the Great Apostle did in a new location - almost invariably - was to go to the Jews: and this in the face of the fact that it was also the Jews who gave him his stiffest opposition. But to deal with the Gentiles it was necessary first to wrestle with a totally foreign mind-set: a world in which strange gods and goddesses ruled the roost; indeed, a world in which the idea of a single deity who was also "righteous" (and did not want sacrifices) was utterly strange. With all the cruelty in the realms of nature and of human nature, how could such a being be?

That the first Christians, all of whom were Jews, did wrestle with the Pagan mind-set is amply proven by the rapid spread of the new faith; but this was not done without much teaching - heavy doses of catechizing - from the Old Testament, the early Church's only Bible.

To the beginnings of this new faith we now turn, but not, I trust, without an humble sense of its immense debt to the old.

NOTES

1. Psalm 22:1-19
2. John 19:24
3. Joel 2:28-32a
4. Isaiah 13:10, Ezekiel 32:7
5. Matthew 24:29, Mark 13:24, Luke 21:25
6. Jeremiah 31:31-34
7. Matthew 26:28, Mark 14:24, Luke 22:20, 1 Corinthians 11:25
8. Romans 11:27, 2 Corinthians 3:6
9. Hebrews 8:8-12, also 10:16-17
10. Isaiah 9:6b
11. Zechariah 9:10b
12. John 4:22b

VIII

A NEW COVENANT

WE HAVE SEEN divine inspiration at work in the Old Testament. In the New Testament, many hold, we touch the Divine Himself. From the Christian point of view, at least, the life, teachings and death of Jesus of Nazareth can be explained in no other manner. The resurrection was inevitable, the ascension a matter of course.

If the Gospel of Mark makes anything apparent, it is that the young Mark was so moved by the suffering and death of this man, that he was converted on the spot. Consider: no beatific vision, no voices from Heaven, no indication of triumph whatsoever: just a man dying in agony on a cross. But in this alone Mark saw God. The words of the centurion were, in reality, his words, "Truly, this man was Son of God!"[1] This, of course, is the great message of the New Testament, namely, that God is love,[2] and Jesus' death, his supreme expression. This was as radical an idea then as it actually is now.

Mark records Jesus' cry of despair, the onlookers' insensitive reaction, the death of the Master, the rending of the veil of the Temple (highly symbolic) and the centurion's response, all in a stark sequence which leaves us in tears.[3] But this is how the life and death of that man was: an unbroken series of hammer blows by an apparently perfect man in an obviously imperfect society. The world has been reeling ever since.

To find a questionable action, an ulterior motive, a human slip recorded of this person in the first three Gospels, one has to look for a damaged watermark on the paper. Of what other person in history can this be said? Further, the accounts ring true. There is certainly no evidence of collusion. As we will see in due course, there is much disagreement as to detail - even contradiction, and great differences in emphases. But in spite of all this, or perhaps because of it, the Nazarene emerges as one who can be explained in no way other than the way in which the centurion (or Mark) explained him to himself.

Who could have thought of such a story? A divine hero who triumphs in death? And who, such teachings? The New Testament alone is proof of divine intervention. It is not susceptible to the usual explanations of literature as reflecting sociological development.

The rulers and elders and scribes of Jerusalem perceived that Peter and John and, presumably, the other disciples, were "uneducated, common men,"[4] and yet from these theoretically unlearned persons has come an incomparable book: to many the most moving piece of literature in existence. The book rehearses the doings and sayings of, and early reflections upon, a man who can only be termed as an interruption in history. Jesus, if he is anything, is unique. If we need a miracle to prove it, we have that miracle already: the New Testament itself. Surely this book is an interruption in the history of literature. It too is unique.

Not everyone sees this at first glance. They see Matthew's and Luke's rather puzzling (and somewhat contradictory) geneologies (tracing Joseph's, not Jesus', family tree!),[5] they see St. Paul's antedeluvian attitude towards women[6] and they see passages of fairly obvious hate in the Book of Revelation. There are other difficulties which we will approach in later chapters. But this is the human side of the book. What is amazing is that there are so few problems of this nature. Even more amazing is the fact that the man whom it celebrates emerges from its pages unscathed: the obvious fulfillment of all that the prophets had spoken - indeed far more than a fulfillment. Jesus, as he is presented in the Gospels, is the apotheosis of the best which had gone before. This, of course, is the meaning of that remarkable episode on the Mount of Transfiguration, wherein Jesus was seen by Peter, James and John as talking with Moses (the Law) and Elijah (the Prophets).[7] It must be remembered that the prophets, magnificent as they were, were nevertheless largely concerned with Israel. They championed Israel's dependence on God for protection. Jesus was concerned with everybody, and championed the dependence of all upon God for fulfillment. After the vision, Peter suggested making three tabernacles to commemorate the event, thereby unwittingly giving Jesus equal status with Moses and Elijah. Hence the voice from the cloud: "This is my beloved Son; listen to *him*." In the vision we are not dealing with equals. Indeed, we are dealing with a new covenant, albeit one based on the old.

It would be absurd at this point to dwell on such difficulties as we find in the New Testament in the face of the majesty of the material presented to us in page after page of the twenty-seven documents which make up the book. There is, however, one difficulty which must be noted here, and that is the plain difficulty of familiarity. Truth is, many of us have heard the major lines of the work so many times that they have lost some of their power to move us. We simply take them for granted. Consider.

There are the Nativity stories and their almost incredible poetry: the *Magnificat* of Mary:

> *My soul magnifies the Lord, and my spirit rejoices in God my Savior, for he has regarded the low estate of his handmaiden ... He has shown strength with his arm, he has scattered the proud in the imagination of their hearts ...*[8]

and the *Benedictus* of Zechariah:

> *Blessed be the Lord God of Israel, for he has visited and redeemed his people, and has raised up a horn of salvation for us in the house of his servant David ... to give light to those who sit in darkness and in the shadow of death, to guide our feet into the way of peace.*[9]

and, finally, the *Nunc Dimithis* of Simeon:

> *Lord, now lettest thou thy servant depart in peace, according to thy word; for mine eyes have seen thy salvation which thou hast prepared in the presence of all peoples, a light for revelation to the Gentiles, and for glory to thy people Israel.*[10]

We read, hear and sing these beautiful words a thousand times and overlook their radical nature, for they represent the bursting on the scene of the universal idea in full flower. At the same time they give credit where credit is due. Likewise the story of the Three Kings, Gentiles all, who came to the Christ-child in Bethlehem of Judea and made their gifts. Cards, creches and pageants commemorate this narrative one Christmas after another, but its significance hardly crosses the thresholds of people's minds.

Putting aside, then, the burden of familiarity, let us proceed into the New Testament, and insofar as we are able in these brief pages, allow the book itself to teach us how to believe.

NOTES

1. Mark 15:39b
2. 1 John 4:8,16
3. Mark 15:33-39
4. Acts 4:13
5. Matthew 1:1-17, Luke 3:23-38
6. See Chapter XVIII
7. Matthew 17:1-8, Mark 9:2-8, Luke 9:28-36
8. Luke 1:46-55
9. Luke 1:68-79
10. Luke 2:29-32

IX

THE TEACHINGS

THE TEACHINGS OF JESUS lay tremendous emphasis on faith, forgiveness and love, these three, and yet we find it impossible to try to confine his teachings to these categories.

In the Gospel of Mark, undoubtedly the first to be written, we go from event to event, with Jesus dealing with people as they come before him and with issues as they arise. There are healings and, in one instance, the connection of these with forgiveness, yes, but we move quickly on to the matter of association with "sinners," i.e., excommunicates from orthodoxy, Matthew among them. There is the question of the Sabbath and Jesus' famous dictum, "The Sabbath was made for man, not man for the Sabbath."[1] To this is added the scathing, "Is it lawful on the Sabbath to do good ...?"[2] There is the accusation that Jesus was "possessed by Beelzebul," the question of who were his brothers, and then parables having to do with a sower, with a seed growing secretly and with the mustard seed. We move on to a storm at sea, a Gerasene demoniac, Jairus'dying daughter, a woman with a hemorrhage and Jesus' rejection by his fellow citizens in Nazareth. From here the narrative moves on in similar fashion from incident to incident.

In other words, in Mark's brief, terse Gospel we go from crisis to crisis, all resulting from Jesus' overwhelming presence, and each one building more tension in the community - and more amazement in the disciples.

There are magnificent teachings, but almost always they are triggered by the situation at hand. When the Pharisees and some of the scribes challenged him because his disciples did not observe the traditional regulations as to washing their hands before eating, he replied,

> *Hear me, all of you, and understand: there is nothing outside a man which by going into him can defile him; but the things which come out of a man are what defile him ... for from within, out of the heart of man, come evil thoughts ... and they defile a man.*[3]

As the end approaches, and its inevitability bears down upon him, there is much about service:

> *"If any one would be first, he must be last of all and servant of all." And he took a child, and put him in the midst of them; and taking him in his arms, he said to them, "Whoever receives one such child in my name receives me; and whoever receives me, receives not me but him who sent me."*[4]

This of course, means love. It turns the usual upside down:

> *You know that those who are supposed to rule over the Gentiles lord it over them, and their great men exercise authority over them. But it shall not be so among you; but whoever would be great among you must be your servant, and whoever would be first among you must be slave of all.*[5]

Most important is the thought that these sentiments have roots of infinite depth:

> *For the Son of man also came not to be served but to serve, and to give his life as a ransom for many.*[6]

In the Gospels of Matthew and of Luke we find far more teachings and far more parables. The Sermon on the Mount all but dominates Matthew's Gospel. Here again it appears to be based largely on the principles of faith, forgiveness and love, but there is much more:

> *Blessed are the poor in spirit, for theirs is the kingdom of heaven. Blessed are those who mourn, for they shall be comforted. Blessed are the meek, for they shall inherit the earth. Blessed are those who hunger and thirst for righteousness, for they shall be satisfied. Blessed are the merciful, for they shall obtain mercy. Blessed are the pure in heart, for they shall see God. Blessed are those who are persecuted for righteousness' sake, for theirs is the kingdom of heaven ...*[7]

And:

> *You have heard that it was said, "You shall love your neighbor and hate your enemy." But I say to you, Love your enemies and pray for those who persecute you, so that you may be sons of your father who is in heaven; for he makes his sun rise on the evil and on the good, and sends his rain on the just and on the unjust ... You, therefore, must be perfect, as your heavenly father is perfect.;*[8]

No higher standard has ever been set for humankind. Perhaps it is no accident that the sermon turns immediately to the subject of prayer. To approach such ideals, surely prayer is needed, and certainly God's forgiveness! Thus the Lord's Prayer, given in this portion of the Sermon, is followed by this reminder:

> *For if you forgive men their trespasses, your heavenly father also will forgive you; but if you do not forgive men their trespasses, neither will your father forgive your trespasses.*[9]

This theme recurs frequently in the Gospels of Matthew and Luke, and we will return to it. The Sermon, however, ends with considerable stress on faith:

> *Therefore I tell you, do not be anxious about your life, what you shall eat or what you shall drink, nor about your body, what you shall put on. Is not life more than food, and the body more than clothing? Look at the birds of the air: they neither sow nor reap; nor gather into barns, and yet your heavenly Father feeds them. Are you not more value than they? ... But seek first his kingdom and his righteousness, and all these things shall be yours as well.*[10]

Shortly after these incomparable words, we read:

> *Ask, and it will be given you; seek, and you will find; knock, and it will be opened to you ... Or what man of you, if his son asks him for a loaf, will he give him a stone? Or if he asks for a fish, will give him a serpent? If you then, who are evil, know how to give good gifts to your children, how much more will your Father who is in heaven give good things to those who ask him?*[11]

In the Lucan account of this saying the final clause is given as:

> *how much more will the heavenly Father give the Holy Spirit to those who ask him?*[12]

Luke's version makes it somewhat clearer what Jesus considered as "good things." This in turn clarifies the intent of "Ask, and it will be given you..." Certain things always are. Many things are not.

The Sermon's words on faith are underlined by an oft-overlooked parable found in the Gospel according to Luke:

And he told them a parable, to the effect that they ought always to pray and not to lose heart. He said, "In a certain city there was a judge who neither feared God nor regarded man; and there was a widow in that city who kept coming to him and saying, 'Vindicate me against my adversary.' For a while he refused; but afterwards he said to himself, 'Though I neither fear God nor regard man, yet because this widow bothers me, I will vindicate her, or she will wear me out by her continual coming.'" And the Lord said, "Hear what the unrighteous judge says. And will not God vindicate his elect, who cry to him day and night? Will he delay long over them? I tell you, he will vindicate them speedily ..."[13]

Lest there be any misunderstanding over the use of the term "elect," there is added these tell-tale words, never to be forgotten:

"Nevertheless, when the Son of Man comes, will he find faith on earth?"

God's purposes are sure, but they still depend on our response - and that is never sure.

So much for faith. There is more, of course, but the point is made. As for forgiveness, nothing matches the breadth of treatment of this subject found in the parable of the prodigal son.[14] Rather long to quote right here, and too familiar for it to be necessary, one still has to note with care that the young man who "squandered his property in loose living" did not come to his senses until he got hungry. Even then his decision to return to his father's house was based on his hope that he could at least get a job. However, whether his confession of sin was sincere or not, his father swept him off his feet and restored him to his accustomed place in the household. This is what enraged the older brother. It also enraged my grandmother. "Perfectly ridiculous!" she used to snort each time that we had the parable in church. "His brother did all the work, and he [i.e., the prodigal] got the fatted calf!" According to Jesus, however, the father had the last word:

> *"It was fitting to make merry and be glad, for this your brother was dead, and is alive; he was lost, and is found."*[15]

Thank God that the Kingdom is not based on "an eye for an eye," but, rather, on grace and forgiveness. For whose motives are one hundred percent pure? The older brother's? Were this demanded, the bells of doom would toll for us all.

To this great story we should add the parable of the unforgiving servant: the man who was forgiven ten thousand talents but would not forgive a debt of one hundred denarii.[16] This tale was told to underline Jesus' answer to Peter's query as to how many times one should forgive a brother:

> *I do not say to you seven times, but seventy times seven.*[17]

The unforgiving servant was ultimately required to pay every last one of his ten thousand talents:

> *So also my heavenly father will do to every one of you, if you do not forgive your brother from your heart.*[18]

Thank God again that we live under grace; but according to Jesus, grace requires grace. Indeed, if we did not forgive one another, the world would soon fall apart.

As to Jesus' emphasis on love, it is found everywhere in the Gospels. "A new commandment I give to you," St. John quotes Jesus as saying, "that you love one another; even as I have loved you, that you love one another."[19] Perhaps no parable underscores this more vividly than the oft-quoted story of the good Samaritan. Here, of course, we are dealing with a no-no in Israelite society. Samaritans were regarded as little better than heathen. Yet Jesus had the temerity to point out that the man fulfilled God's commandment, while the priest and the Levite did not. The Samaritan took care of the wounded stranger, even assumed future responsibility, while the holy men of Israel "passed by on the other side."[20]

Lest there be any doubt as to the ultimate importance of love, we have the great parable of the Last Judgment, found almost immediately before the Last Supper in the Gospel according to St. Matthew:

> *When the Son of man comes in his glory, and all the angels with him, then he will sit on his glorious throne. Before him will be gathered all the nations, and he will separate them one from another as a shepherd separates the sheep from the goats, and he will place the sheep at his right hand, but the goats at the left. Then the King will say to those at his right hand, "Come, O blessed of my Father, inherit the kingdom prepared for you from the foundation of the world; for I was hungry and you gave me food, I was thirsty and you gave me drink, I was a stranger and you welcomed me, I was naked and you clothed me, I was sick and you visited me, I was in prison and you came to me." Then the righteous will answer him, "Lord, when did we see thee hungry and feed thee, or thirsty and give thee drink? And when did we see thee a stranger and welcome thee, or naked and clothe thee? And when did we see thee sick or in prison and visit thee?" And the King will answer them, "Truly I say to you, as you did it to one of the least of these my brethren, you did it to me."*[21]

The tables are then turned on the goats, who did not do these things, and as a result, they are cast out. (Of that, more anon.)

The point to be noted most of all, I think, is that the righteous were unaware of their righteousness. They simply were merciful people. What they had done "to the least of these my brethren" they had done only because they had wanted to do it: a point to be remembered by those who strive for prizes. Which takes us back to the Sermon on the Mount wherein we read:

> *Not every one who says to me, "Lord, Lord," shall enter the kingdom of heaven, but he who does the will of my Father who is in heaven. On that day many will say to me, "Lord, Lord, did we not prophesy in your name, and cast out demons in your name, and do many mighty works in your name? And then will I declare to them, "I never knew you; depart from me, you evildoers."*[22]

Obviously, these people were looking for a pay-off.

Truth is that we, who are not at all like our heavenly Father, are called by Jesus to be exactly like him. To some, this is the "bad news" of the New Testament. The "good news," however, is the assumption which is made throughout its astonishing pages that God freely gives the Holy Spirit to those who ask him, and that this turns them around.

So much for the three great emphases in Jesus' teachings: faith, forgiveness and love. But lest we think that this is all, we come hard against a parable like this one:

> *Two men went up into the temple to pray, one a Pharisee and the other a tax collector. The Pharisee stood and prayed thus with himself, "God, I thank thee that I am not like other men, extortioners, unjust, adulterers, or even like this tax collector. I fast twice a week,*

> *I give tithes of all that I get." But the tax collector, standing far off, would not even lift up his eyes to heaven, but beat his breast, saying, "God, be merciful to me a sinner!" I tell you, this man went down to his house justified rather than the other; for every one who exalts himself will be humbled, but he who humbles himself will be exalted.*[23]

There is something absolutely basic in these words. Faith in oneself may be all right up to a point, but in the long run faith in oneself, minus God, is faith in an illusion. Until we realize this stark fact, there is little which God can do to help us.

Jesus, in no sense a pedant, dealt with life as it presented itself to him. Consequently, his teachings have a curious way of covering so much of life as it presents itself to us. Further, life has so many facets that it seldom yields to absolute categories or, indeed, even to consistency. Neither does the Master. Hence we have sayings and parables which cannot be placed under any one of the three main heads which we have chosen. Nor can all of them be that readily understood.

The important item here is the sublimity of just about all of the material before us. We cannot be surprised that there is hardly a line in the Gospels which has not become a household word in this part of the world or in that. Indeed, Jesus' teachings have not seldom been taken as indications of his unique identity. Such being the case, we might well be led to wonder whether the same can be said about his life and death. To these we now turn.

NOTES

1. Mark 2:27
2. Mark 3:4a
3. Mark 7:14,15,21a,23b
4. Mark 9:35-37
5. Mark 10:42-44 (See Chapter XVI of this work.)
6. Mark 10:45
7. Matthew 5:3-10
8. Matthew 5:43-45, 48
9. Matthew 6:14-15
10. Matthew 6:25-26, 33
11. Matthew 7:7,9-11
12. Luke 11:13b
13. Luke 18:1-8
14. Luke 15:11-32
15. Luke 15:32
16. Matthew 18:23-35
17. Matthew 18:22
18. Matthew 18:35
19. John 13:34
20. Luke 10:25-37
21. Matthew 25:31-40
22. Matthew 7:21-23
23. Luke 18:10:14

X

THE LIFE

IN THE CARE OF the curators of Monticello there is a pencilled New Testament, once part of the Bible of Thomas Jefferson, now the object of curiosity for the visitors to his beautiful house in Charlottesville, Virginia. What Mr. Jefferson did was to pencil out those passages which he could not accept. In general, the censored portions have to do with Jesus' life, the uncensored, with his teachings.

With enormous respect for "the sage of Monticello" and also for his right to do whatever he wished for himself, one must nevertheless observe that for most of us such a selection destroys the evidence before it is presented. We all know that people are not ordinarily born of virgins, do not usually walk on water, are not expected to feed 5000 on five loaves and two fish and have not customarily risen from the dead.

Without getting into the Gospel of John, which we will do in due course, the controversial events found in the first three (the "Synoptic") Gospels do stand up well under close inspection when we take them case by case. As far as this author is concerned, Jesus' doings, like his teachings, speak for themselves.

Immediately there is the matter of his birth. That Matthew's and Luke's accounts of his being born of a virgin should present a stumbling-block to many minds appears to me as unnecessary and unfortunate. In both instances we have passages of almost incredible beauty - highly appropriate to the life which they introduce. One should hesitate before smashing a stained-glass window.

To me, at least, it is just a little bit sickening when otherwise sensible people scotch these masterpieces of literature with lectures on freshman biology. What? Is God unable to do what these writers say that he did? And if Jesus was indeed the Son of God, would it be against the much-touted "laws of nature" for him to be born as Matthew and Luke state that he was?

Nobody believes that Jesus was the Son of God because he was born of a virgin. At least nobody should. It is only after a thorough consideration of his life and teachings that we can come to a conclusion of divinity, and it is only then that we may accept what we read at the beginning. It is perhaps for this reason that no mention whatever is made of the virgin birth in the other writings of the New Testament. Not once is it offered as a "proof."

Moving on to the adult Jesus, it quickly becomes apparent that he possessed a magnetism which could be resisted only in his home town.[1] Everywhere else that he went he drew great crowds - from the very beginning.[2] Likewise he drew instant hostility from the entrenched religious powers.[3] His very existence was a challenge. "We never saw anything like this!"[4] was the customary reaction to his presence. Equally telling are the words of his disciples: "Everyone is searching for you."[5]

By far the most frequent "doings" in Jesus' ministry, beyond his teachings, were his acts of healing. In the Synoptic Gospels, these were almost inevitably connected by the Master with one of two conditions: his forgiveness or the suppliant's faith. The one exception to this rule was the casting out of "unclean spirits," a frequent occurrence in his ministry.

As to these latter instances, mental illness and epilepsy were, in those unscientific times, ascribed to "the hosts of darkness," who took hold of certain people and either made them violent or periodically threw them to the ground, foaming. If Jesus were human, and the New Testament everywhere avers that he was, then he had the knowledge of his day and went along with it. Certainly he said nothing to change the popular concepts as to the origins of these maladies. But his towering personality and penetrating concern were enough, presumably, to effect the cure of any number of these people.

With the others, it was obviously a matter of releasing the suppliant from guilt, or of effecting a cure through faith. Thus we have him asking the scribes, "Which is easier to say to the paralytic, 'Your sins are forgiven,' or to say, 'Rise, take up your pallet and walk'?"[6] On the other hand, to the woman whom he healed of a hemorrhage, he said, "Daughter, your faith has made you well; go in peace, and be healed of your disease."[7] There are few doctors today who would question either one of these so-called "miracles."

Not every one has "the gift of healing," nor do many have even an approximation of the personality of Jesus. But this is not to say that these two phenomena did not exist in one person. Mr. Jefferson used his pencil too quickly.

In the Synoptic Gospels there are two instances of Jesus bringing someone presumed to be dead back to life. All three Synoptics tell how he revived the daughter of Jairus,[8] a ruler of a synagogue, and Luke relates a similar happening to the son of a widow in Nain.[9] Here are two cases which anyone can pencil out with impunity if one wishes to. Personally, I have no difficulty with either. It is plain that Jesus did not make a practice of this sort of thing, else he would have been at it constantly. These particular occasions were surrounded by conditions of extreme pathos. Their message appears to have been Jesus' compassion rather than his miraculous powers. In the case of Jairus' daughter, Mark's account ends with: "And he strictly charged them that no one should know this, and told them to give her something to eat."

Which brings us to a most important item, namely, the famous "messianic secret."

The Synoptics tell us how the Pharisees "came and began to argue with him, seeking from him a sign from heaven to test him." Jesus "sighed deeply in spirit, and said, 'Why does this generation seek a sign? Truly I say to you, no sign shall be given to this generation.'"[10] This, of course, was a foreshadowing of a similar question hurled at a man dying on a cross. Jesus' complete answer is found in Matthew and Luke:

> *... no sign shall be given ... except the sign of Jonah. For as Jonah became a sign to the men of Nineveh, so will the Son of man be to this generation ... The men of Nineveh will arise at the judgment with this generation and condemn it; for they repented at the preaching of Jonah, and behold, something greater than Jonah is here.*[11]

These words are, in fact, the key to understanding much of what Jesus said and did, and, equally important, much of what he did *not* say and do.

Why did he *not* come down from the cross? Why did he *not* appear before his enemies after his resurrection? Indeed, why does he *not* appear to us now? The answer to all of these questions is contained in the cryptic reference to Jonah. If what Jesus stood for, preached and lived does not appeal to people without signs and wonders, neither will they appeal with them.

Jesus concluded one of his great parables with a similar observation. When the rich man in hell asked Abraham to send Lazarus from his bosom to warn the rich man's brothers, Abraham replied, "If they do not hear Moses and the Prophets, neither will they be convinced if some one should rise from the dead."[12] In considering the resurrection of Jesus, we should remember this remark.

It seems that Jesus was always aware of the danger of being regarded as a miracle man, a wonder worker, and *therefore* the Messiah. He came illustrating a way of life, an example of character - indeed, a revelation of the nature of God. Either we respond to this or we do not. Thus, until the end, it fell only to those who did respond to be told the messianic secret. Further, at the end, only those bound to him in that tight Galilean fellowship had the highly emotional experience of seeing him after his death. The one recorded exception to this was, of course, Saul of Tarsus, but *not* the High Priest and *not* Pontius Pilate. You cannot scare people into changing their values.

In instance after instance, Jesus, when he healed someone, would endeavor to silence those involved:

> *And he charged them to tell no one; but the more he charged them, the more zealously they proclaimed it. And they were astonished beyond measure, saying, "He has done all things well; he even makes the deaf hear and the dumb speak."*[13]

But it does no good to regard Jesus as the Messiah unless one first sees him as such because of what he is rather than because of what he does. Wisdom always boils down to a sense of values, and values are what Jesus came to represent.

And then there is the matter of faith. Do we believe that values lie at the heart of the universe? With all of its catastrophes and cruelties, is the world of nature and human nature undergirded by lofty values? If the Creator is an engineer, a chemist and a mathematician, is he also characterized by such an attitude as love? This is not always easy to believe.

I often think of that unforgettable scene recorded in Matthew, Mark and John when the disciples were rowing into a night gale on the Sea of Galilee, and he came to them across the water:

> *He meant to pass by them, but when they saw him walking on the sea they thought it was a ghost, and cried out; for they all saw him and were terrified. But immediately he spoke to them and said, 'Take heart, it is I; Have no fear.' And he got into the boat with them and the wind ceased. And they were utterly astounded, for they did not understand about the loaves ...*[14]

How many recovering alcoholics understand this passage! Here again is one which Mr. Jefferson pencilled out too soon. It even underlines our confusion, our mixed motives, our partial faith. But the point is that the disciples did not let him pass by, and he entered their boat - and the gale ceased.

And there is that oblique reference to the loaves. In all four Gospels, and in two of them twice, we have accounts of "miraculous" feedings of the multitudes - the multitudes which had followed Jesus to the point of fainting. Without laboring an explanation, we simply turn to Jesus' dictum in the Sermon: "Therefore do not be anxious, saying, 'What shall we eat?' or 'What shall we drink?'... But seek first his kingdom and his righteousness, and all these things shall be yours as well."[15] It is indeed a matter of faith. If we really seek the Lord, should we worry?

What actually happened when five loaves and two fish fed 5000 people and yielded twelve baskets of leftovers, we will not know for certain this side of Jordan. All that we do know is that this event, or events, was (were) recorded six times: more than any other event in Jesus' earthly life.

There are esoteric explanations of the two feedings in Mark - repeated in Matthew (Luke and John record only the first one) - explanations involving the mystic meanings of the numbers of loaves, fish and baskets, but I have always found these explanations difficult to credit. Mark, whose material appears to be the original for the others, is, if he is anything, simple and direct. This is what makes his Gospel so powerful. He is not susceptible to explanations of any kind. What he writes is obviously what he considers as history. Perhaps the only acceptable explanation which we can give to these extraordinary events is found in the simple fact that we are dealing with an extraordinary man.

There were numerous other "doings" of the Master which were the objects of Mr. Jefferson's censorious pencil - doings which nevertheless pass the test of teaching some important truth other than the divine identity of their doer. Alas, the great man of Charlottesville overlooked this important point. The age of reason had apparently obscured the poetry of the thoughts and actions of the Nazarene, just as the age of science is apt to obscure them for us.

Illustrating exactly this point, there comes to mind an incident in the life of Jesus which is as important as any which we have considered, and as neglected as any, even though it appears in varying forms in all four Gospels. Mark writes:

> *And while he was at Bethany in the house of Simon the leper, as he sat at table, a woman came with an alabaster jar of ointment of pure nard, very costly, and she broke the jar and poured it over his head. But there were some who said to themselves indignantly, "Why was this ointment thus wasted? For this ointment might have been sold for more than three hundred denarii, and given to the poor." And they reproached her. But Jesus said, "Let her alone; why do you trouble her? She has done a beautiful thing to me. For you always have the poor with you, and whenever you will, you can do good to them; but you will not always have me. She has done what she could; she has anointed my body beforehand for burying. And truly, I say to you, wherever the gospel is preached in the whole world, what she has done will be told in memory of her."*[16]

There is no more telling poetry than this. We have here a singing reminder that responding to Jesus does not simply consist in pious works of charity. As St. Paul put it later, it also involves "psalms and hymns and spiritual songs"[17] - expressions of thankfulness and devotion, expressions, indeed, which cannot be stifled. They may take the form of literature, of art and architecture, of music, or even of juggling before the altar. But such expressions further not only our own emotions but those of others as well. When Jesus declared that the woman's act would always be remembered, he spoke a truth which attaches to a million such acts and works: to cathedrals and symphonies, to paintings and poems, to books and bronzes, all of which make of this world a New Jerusalem.

Alas, there are always those who, for reasons of their own, oppose these things, as well as other principles for which Jesus stood. Opposition to Jesus began early in his ministry and grew more intense as time went on. Which brings us to the passion, the unfolding of which proved for many to be the turning point in history and the summation of as complete a revelation of God as is possible in this finite world.

NOTES

1. Mark 6:1-6
2. Mark 1:32-33
3. Mark 3:6
4. Mark 2:12b
5. Mark 1:37b
6. Mark 2:9
7. Mark 5:34
8. Mark 5:21-24, 35-43 and parallels
9. Luke 7:11-17
10. Mark 8:11-12
11. Luke 11:29b-30,32
12. Luke 16:31 (See Chapter XVII of this work)
13. Mark 7:36-37
14. Mark 6:48b-52a
15. Matthew 6:31a,33
16. Mark 14:3-9
17. Colossians 3:16b

XI

THE DEATH

SINCE THE POPULAR CONCEPT of the day was that the Messiah would "restore the kingdom to Israel,"[1] Jesus, who had no such objective in mind, leaned over backwards to forestall any premature recognition of his messiahship. As far as he was concerned, no recognition was desirable which did not include a recognition of the sort of messiah that he was. We have already noted his frequent injunctions to suppliants that they "tell no one" of healings or of other extraordinary acts which might be construed as being of a messianic nature. But his evident purpose was still to fulfill the role of the Messiah. As time began to run out on him because of the hostility of the establishment, he made up his mind to declare himself, and to do it in such a manner as (1.) to capture the utmost attention and (2.) to convey the proper clues as to the nature of his mission.

For these twin purposes the famous prophecy in Zechariah (See Chapter VI) was made to order. Hence Zion's king came to her "triumphant and victorious," yes, but also "humble and riding on an ass."[2] The occasion: the first day of the week preceding the Passover, a week during which pilgrims would begin to throng the Holy City for the feast. To us, that day is remembered as "Palm Sunday."

The welcome accorded the Master as he came reflected the fame which had gone before him, the respect in which he was held and the confidence of multitudes that he was indeed the long-awaited Messiah. Looking back on this startling event and its sequel, we can only judge that the

Synoptic Gospels have, if anything, understated the extent of Jesus' influence. For not only did Jesus receive a tumultous welcome on that first day, but also he subsequently accomplished the clearing of the Temple of its tawdry traffic in sacrificial animals and "sacred" coin. This act was as radical and as dangerous a measure as anyone in that society could possibly have undertaken. The sale of sacrificial animals and the trading of Roman money, invalid in the Temple, for Hebrew coinage, invalid outside, provided important revenue for the Temple authorities. At the same time there was no real reason why the sacrifices could not be bought at the market or the money exchanged for more reasonable fees. The fact that Jesus cleared the Temple of these monopolistic practices and then continued to hold court there for four consecutive days speaks louder of his hold on the populace than any of the rather modest encomiums found in the Synoptics. Even with the authorities in a position to stir up the many pilgrims, some of whom were making a once-in-a-lifetime visit to the Temple, it was still necessary for them to endeavor to sieze Jesus at night, if they were to sieze him at all.

It has often been stated that those who greeted him with "Hosannas" on Sunday cried out, "Crucify him!" on Friday. Doubtless, there were some who did fall into this category. It was indeed the popular concept that the Messiah would restore Israel's glory, and disappointment in this respect must have turned some against the Nazarene. It is my opinion that this is precisely what led Judas to betray his Master. He, himself, felt betrayed. He had followed this man around for many months, confident that he would ultimately introduce the long-expected era of Hebrew ascendancy. And now Jesus had apparently lost his nerve.

Fact is, all of the disciples fell into this category. As we have seen, even after his resurrection they were still thinking in terms of the restoration of the Israelite kingdom. All of which only reflects how deeply ingrained "civil religion" can become. After months with the Master and his universal attitude and teachings, the disciples were still as prejudiced as any super-patriot ever was.

But there was a difference, and that difference lay in their deep devotion to Jesus himself. Even Judas, when he reflected on what he had done, went out and hanged himself. (Not that that accomplished anything.)

In the meantime the city as a whole appears to have accepted Jesus. Further, there was evidently considerable public sympathy with what he had done in the Temple. Not only did he "hold court" there, uttering some of his most famous teachings, but he also "would not allow any one to carry anything through the Temple."[3] The Temple, as far as he was concerned, was a house of prayer, and "for all the nations."[4] The authorities found themselves in a very embarrassing situation, about which there was nothing obvious which they could do.

Thus I very much question whether there were many from the Palm Sunday crowd calling for his death on Good Friday. Most of the latter people were assuredly pilgrims, largely unacquainted with the man from Nazareth, and thoroughly misinformed about him. "We heard him say, 'I will destroy this temple that is made with hands, and in three days I will build another, not made with hands.'"[5] We can well imagine the source and passage of that little nugget - and its effect on a pious pilgrim. On Friday morning the Jerusalemites were either in their homes, as most would be that early in the day, or going about their business.

Somewhere amidst a host of campers, Jesus and his disciples had their own camp outside the city. To find it, especially at night, would have been like finding the proverbial needle in a haystack. Hence the need for a betrayer.

The story of the Passion is so familiar that we often miss the issues and, consequently, the impact. For this writer at least, its unbelievable power flows from the stark contrast between divinity and humanity when the two are locked in controversy.

One is often tempted to speculate. What would have happened had Judas not caved in? What would have happened had the High Priest taken a different attitude? What would have happened had Pontius Pilate refused to be intimidated? The answer to all of these questions is, I fear, simply that humanity, as it constitutes itself everywhere, is so compromised with selfishness and false self-esteem, that it cannot long abide the presence of one as selfless as Jesus of Nazareth. Were he to return today, perhaps he would receive more deference, but my guess is that it would not be long before his person would become unbearable to a great many people.

And it was not only the priests and council, not only the stirred-up crowd and Pilate, but it was also Judas, who betrayed him, Peter, who denied him, and all of his disciples, who forsook him. When the chips are down, humanity inevitably collapses. *"There is no health in us."* And here is exactly where religion must begin. Without divine forgiveness and a liberal supply of the Unseen Power, we are nothing. And how nothing we really are!

How ridiculous the scene of his arrest! Jesus himself pointed this out: "Have you come out as against a robber, with swords and clubs to capture - me?"[6] But such was the measure of his stature. Yes, they could have seized him - readily - in the Temple, but, as Mark twice points out, they "feared the multitude."[7] It was for this reason, of course, that they tried him at night (which was illegal), took him madly before Pilate (who alone could pronounce the death sentence) and got the whole messy business over before nine o'clock. But at the bottom of all this was the evident fact that they feared the man himself, and were acting out of that desperation which invades the soul when one's basic motives are brought glaringly into question. Jesus had broken no laws, made no threats and, in proclaiming his messiahship, issued no ultimatums. As far as blasphemy was concerned, he had not committed it, in spite of the High Priest's accusation. After all, they all looked for the Messiah to come, and could hardly expect such a one to deny his identity when he came. The awful truth remains, they had to get rid of him.

The story of the Passion is somewhat relieved by two incidents during those final twenty hours.

One was the supper in which Jesus, according to the Synoptics, ate the Passover with his disciples. In his breaking the bread and passing the cup, he left with them - and with us - a perpetual reminder of his sacrifice for our sakes. As far as I know, all who call themselves Christians observe this rite to this day.

The other incident is recorded only by St. Luke. He tells of "a great multitude of the people, and of women who bewailed and lamented him." (Note: no mention of the disciples.) These were following him on the "Via

Dolorosa" to Golgotha. What Jesus said to them also continues to ring in our ears: "Daughters of Jerusalem, do not weep for me, but weep for yourselves and for your children ... for if they do this when the wood is green, what will happen when it is dry?"[8] Alas, the history of nations provides the ghastly answer to this searching question.

Item: the presence of sympathizing women to the very end, even though they were in less danger than the disciples might have been, nevertheless provides a blessed relief in an otherwise totally black story. According to the Synoptic Gospels, some of that gender, which was definitely *not* running the world of those times, were alone supportive at his death and, marvelously, alone first at his resurrection. One is often constrained to wonder whether women are of the same species as men.

There is no passage anywhere in all of literature which can compare in power with Mark's account of the Passion. He first takes us from the supper to Gethsemane. There Jesus, sensing the approach of the posse from the High Priest, asks three of his disciples to keep watch while he prays. Three times he returns to find them asleep. When the posse does arrive, another disciple, Judas, indentifies him with a kiss. All the other disciples disappear. Jesus is then hauled before the Council, where the witnesses against him disagree. The High Priest loses patience and bursts out with the risky question, "Are you the Christ, the Son of the Blessed?"[9] Jesus flatly declares that he is. This, illogically and illegally, is used to condemn him. He is then received by the guards "with blows."[10] In the meantime, Peter, who had summoned enough courage to come back and into the courtyard, refuses to admit that he ever knew him. Jesus is then hustled to Pontius Pilate, the Roman Governor, who alone possessed civil authority. There Jesus is accused of trying to be a king and thereby threaten Roman rule. (How hypocritical could his accusers get? They all hated Roman rule.) Pilate, knowing full well how hypocritical all this was, endeavors to release him. When he finds that this will cause a disturbance of some consequence, he blandly gives in. To make matters worse (and doubtless to pacify the local authorities), he has Jesus flogged. The soldiers take full advantage of their opportunity (and of their disdain for "the natives") and add insult to injury.

The death-march comes next, and the help given to the failing Master by a passer-by, one Simon of Cyrene, albeit involuntarily. The crucifixion then takes place. Even Mark, objective as he was, is unable to write out the details of this horror. He simply states, "And they crucified him ..."[11] : the most important happening in human history - in four words.

The parting of the garments by the soldiers, the noting of the hour - the third, the sardonic inscription - "The King of the Jews" - and the crucifixion of the two robbers (Imagine!) follow, then the mocking of the onlookers, including the chief priests and scribes. All of this is recorded without comment. As if any were needed! Already overwhelmed, we come to what I hold to be the most moving passage in all literature:

> *And when the sixth hour had come, there was darkness over the whole land until the ninth hour. And at the ninth hour Jesus cried with a loud voice, "E´lo-i, E´lo-i, la´-ma sabach-tha´ni?" which means, "My God, my God, why hast thou forsaken me?" And some of the bystanders hearing it said, "Behold, he is calling Eli´jah." And one ran and, filling a sponge full of vinegar, put it on a reed and gave it to him to drink, saying, "Wait, let us see whether Eli´-jah will come to take him down." And Jesus uttered a loud cry, and breathed his last.*

And the curtain of the temple was torn in two, from top to bottom. And when the centurion saw that he thus breathed his last, he said, "Truly this man was son of God!"[12]

Seven "Ands," seven staggering statements.

There is an old spiritual which begins, "Were you there when they crucified my Lord? Oh! Sometimes it causes me to tremble ..." Mark has put us there, and indeed it does cause us to tremble. The utter contrasts! Here was perhaps the only man ever to do nothing worthy of punishment now suffering the cruelest of all punishments, and being ridiculed and derided to the end.

If our intellects fail us, surely our emotions respond to those final words, "My God, my God, why hast thou forsaken me?" Perhaps we can understand, "My God, my God," but how can our minds understand Jesus' feeling forsaken by God, especially when he had prophesied that this is exactly what would happen? If our intellects are ultimately able to catch up with our emotions, perhaps they will point out to us that during those six endless hours which Jesus spent in utter agony on the cross, there was absolutely nothing which, given the Divine Nature, the Father in Heaven could do. As we have noted in "The Green Pastures," he could only lean on his roll-top desk, his eyes cast down, while his angels wrung their hands. His Son was on his own.

The fact is that the cry of despair was, for Mark, the culmination of a sequence of events which was for him a complete revelation of the Deity. Offhand, one might think that Mark's account was of a man beaten, degraded and humiliated by some rather powerful officials. Nothing could be further from the truth. What we actually see is a rock of incredible grace and dignity around which a lot of little people manage to humiliate themselves and, I fear, most of their fellow mortals.

The cry of despair, the only word from the cross which Mark records (the other Gospels record six more) is at once a sign of the authenticity of Mark's Gospel and an evidence of the reality of Jesus' humanity. And there is a question about it: Was this despair for Jesus himself or for those around him? With them he could accomplish nothing. Their total insensitivity, their entirely obtuse reaction - these could indicate only an utterly hopeless state of mind. The cry, indeed, elicited another absurd response, "He is calling Elijah!", and a crude offer of vinegar, as if that might keep him alive until Elijah came. This met with another cry from the cross, an inarticulate one, and Jesus "breathed his last."

The end had come - precipitately. But it turned out to be very far indeed from the end. Here is where we come to the whole point of Mark's account. The end was actually the beginning. It was precisely *then* that the curtain of the Temple, that symbol of the veil between God and humankind, "was torn in two, from top to bottom." Likewise it was precisely *then* that the centurion burst forth with, "Truly this man was Son of God!"

Need we say it? Love, perfect love, had at last been revealed.

Edward Gibbon, the great eighteenth century historian, assumed that the darkness, which Mark refers to near the end, covered the whole earth. Perhaps it did. Perhaps it still does. If there is any light at all, it is to be found on that distant cross. It is a light with an intensity all its own. St. John wrote that it is the "true light that enlightens every man ..."[13] I am sure that it does. The question, however, is not the reality of the light, but just how much "every man" allows it to guide him. But the question before us here is a different one. It is simply this: As to that light, can there be any doubt about its source?

NOTES

1. Acts 1:6b
2. Zechariah 9:9
3. Mark 11:16
4. Mark 11:17
5. Mark 14:58
6. Mark 14:48
7. Mark 11:18, 12:12
8. Luke 23:28, 31
9. Mark 14:61b
10. Mark 14:65b
11. Mark 15:24a
12. Mark 15:33-39
13. John 1:9a

XII

THE EMPTY TOMB

THE RESURRECTION of Jesus of Nazareth was unnecessary; it was also inevitable: unnecessary because his divinity had already been established, inevitable because he was divine. Having said this, one must nevertheless admit that the resurrection was necessary for the disciples. They were so demoralized by the crucifixion - and by their own behavior - that something was needed to assure them that they were forgiven, and needed also to restore their spirits. It is difficult enough to believe in forgiveness, but when you feel that you have cruelly wronged the Lord himself, it is all but impossible. It was the resurrection which turned the disciples around, and precipitately.

People frequently ask now, as they undoubtedly did then, Why does the risen Lord not appear to us? St. John parries this thrust at the original end of his Gospel. He quotes the risen Jesus as saying to the doubting Thomas, "Have you believed because you have seen me? Blessed are those who have not seen and yet believe."[1]

Truth is, none of us, or of the others of those times, has had the relationship which the disciples had had with the man, Jesus, nor the emotional state which this must have created - particularly during the passion. For them to have experienced him after his death seems to me like the most natural thing that ever happened: natural for them, and certainly natural for him. However frustrated they may have felt within themselves, truth stared them in the face.

We have, actually, five accounts of the resurrection. They are found in the four Gospels and in St. Paul's first letter to the Corinthians. They are of extraordinary interest.

First of all, one notes the similarities which run through most if not all of them: the third day, the women, the empty tomb (and it was empty - even the authorities admitted that),[2] the strange announcing personages, the limited number of witnesses, their utter surprise and the intermittent nature of the experience.

Even more notable, however, are the differences. With regard to places, times, people, and statements, there is much disagreement, so much so that it is impossible to synchronize them to make a continuous narrative, even in the most hypothetical manner. The fact that much of Mark's account is obviously missing is of little significance in the face of such varying testimony as we already possess.

(Mark's Gospel ends in an unresolved sentence. He speaks of the women fleeing from the empty tomb, " for trembling and astonishment had come upon them; and they said nothing to any one, for they were afraid of..."[3] whatever else of chapter sixteen appears in various versions of the New Testament was added later to supply the deficiency. Alas, the end of the original scroll was, apparently, torn off.)

Thus we are faced with such questions as: Did the women see a young man in the tomb, as Mark tells us, or is Matthew correct in declaring that they saw an angel seated outside on the stone? Was he seen for forty days, as Luke asserts in Acts, or for but one or two, as Matthew indicates and, indeed, as Luke says in his Gospel? Did he ascend in Galilee, as Matthew states, or in Bethany, as Luke writes?

How foolish to see in these discrepancies anything but the evidence of sincere reporting! They represent exactly what one would expect of different people telling of any exciting event. The testimony given in the case of an accident invariably presents contradictions. In fact, it is almost a rule that when all witnesses agree, there arises the suspicion of collusion. Add to this rather mundane observation the simple fact that the resurrection accounts were written down years after the event, and it becomes rather amazing that there are not even wider discrepancies.

Be that as it may, I have long felt that there is much more to the differences in the resurrection accounts than simply the normal lapses in human memory.

Language is based on experience. When we tell someone of a particularly dramatic sunrise, we can do so with a measure of success because that person has seen other sunrises. When we enthuse over a certain church service, our friends can appreciate our enthusiasm because they also have been involved in similar services. The effectiveness of words depends largely upon common experience.

But the resurrection of Jesus stands alone in history. We tend to forget this. Nothing like it had ever happened before. There are not even any claims to such an occurrence. Nobody had thought of such a thing. Nor has anything remotely resembling it been reported - or alleged - ever since. We have to remind ourselves that it was not merely the restoring of human life to a person, as in the case of Jairus' daughter or of the son of the widow of

Nain, or of Lazarus. Jesus was not restored to mortal life as we know it. He came and went, came and went, in a peculiar way. In short, his resurrection was unique. There was, therefore, no language with which to describe it. If Jesus rose from the dead, inadequate descriptions of the event would be precisely what we would expect - extremely inadequate.

Let us press the point still further. Witnessing the resurrection was apparently a very personal experience. There are three tell-tale words in this respect in Matthew's account of Jesus' appearance to the eleven in Galilee. He writes, " And when they saw him they worshipped him..." Clear enough. But then he adds those three words: "but some doubted."[4] Obviously, recognizing the risen Lord was not quite like recognizing a friend in the market place. In four recorded instances, followers encountering the risen Lord did not initially recognize him. All of which removes the resurrection experience even further from the realm of everyday language. One begins to wonder whether it could really be described at all.

Which brings us to a highly significant item - an item about which this writer used to puzzle as a child. This, the supreme experience in the lives of Jesus' original followers - this is the very one which receives the briefest treatment in their ultimate record: one chapter in each of the first three Gospels, two in the fourth. In fact, the second of John's two chapters was quite evidently wrung from the writer some time after he had finished his book. And Matthew's one chapter consists of a bare twenty verses. Why?

In the course of a lifetime I have come to realize that the extreme reticence on the subject of the resurrection actually speaks volumes. In the first place, as we have already noted, it had become the assumption of the Synoptics that belief in Jesus should not be the result of signs and wonders.

Such belief, obviously, could not be based on conviction but only on fear. Thus belief in the divinity of the man from Nazareth was not solicited by the miracle of the resurrection. As with the virgin birth, so with the resurrection, belief was to be based on the miracle of Jesus himself. After all, anyone can write a miracle story. Who could even dream of the life, teachings and death of Jesus of Nazareth?

But we are not through with this matter. Some of us have had our own mysterious and deep experiences. Most of us have learned not to speak of them, except perhaps to our most intimate friends. For one thing, it is very difficult to describe them. For another, we do not wish to expose them to ridicule: "George is seeing visions again!" Think of how the disciples must have already felt before the scoffers of their time. "Well, have you seen the King of the Jews lately?" Jesus - blessed Jesus - to be crucified again?

Perhaps we are more than fortunate to have the accounts which we actually have. but there they are with all their agreements and disagreements, their agonizingly inadequate descriptions, their extreme brevity and their maddening lack of precision.

Undoubtedly the most puzzling single feature is Luke's own contradiction of himself. As we have already noticed, in his Gospel he confines the resurrection events to a single day, at the end of which Jesus "parted from them," and, according to some ancient manuscripts, "was carried into heaven."[5] Whereas in his account in Acts, the ascension into Heaven takes place after forty days of appearances to "the apostles whom he had chosen."[6] (Paul states that he appeared to 500.)[7]

I think it meet and right to point out that we are dealing with something more than a searching of memories or a certain carelessness as to relatively unimportant detail. (The New Testament seldom tells us anything more than that which we need to know.) We are here dealing with an unprecedented impingement of eternity on time. The experience of the moment was actually an experience of all moments and of no moment. It was overwhelming. It embraced one's entire life. If there is any "proof" of the resurrection, it is found in what it did to those who experienced it.

Luke tells of that unbelievably naive question asked of Jesus by the disciples almost at the minute of his ascension: "Lord, will you at this time restore the kingdom to Israel?"[8] The most inappropriate farewell in history! After all that he had said and done... Jesus' answer represents the ultimate in understanding, patience and tact: "It is not for you to know times or seasons which the Father has fixed by his own authority. But you shall receive power when the Holy Spirit has come upon you; and you shall be my witnesses in Jerusalem and in all Judea *and Samaria and to the end of the earth*."[9]

And, at extreme cost to themselves, they were just such witnesses.

Having said all this, one still has to step aside and let the resurrection passages speak for themselves. To prove that they do this with incredible power we need to quote but one. This one is found in the Gospel according to St. Luke.[10]

Jesus had been crucified. The disciples had been shattered. The gloom was unfathomable. The early morning mists had been somewhat dispelled when certain women of Jesus' little band found the tomb empty.

Luke continues the account:

That very day two of them were going to a village named Emmaus, about seven miles from Jerusalem, and talking with each other about all these things that had happened. While they were talking and discussing together, Jesus himself drew near and went with them. But their eyes were kept from recognizing him. And he said to them, " What is this conversation which you are holding with each other as you walk?" And they stood still, looking sad. Then one of them, named Cleopas, answered him, "Are you the only visitor to Jerusalem who does not know the things that have happened there in these days?" And he said to them, "What things?" And they said to him, "Concerning Jesus of Nazareth, who was a prophet mighty in deed and word before God and all the people, and how our chief priests and rulers delivered him up to be condemned to death, and crucified him. But we had hoped that he was the one to redeem Israel. Yes, and besides all this, it is now the third day since this happened. Moreover, some women of our company amazed us. They were at the tomb early in the morning and did not find his body; and they came back saying that they had even seen a vision of angels, who said that he was alive. Some of those who were with us went to the tomb , and found it just as the women had said; but him they did not see." And he said to them, "O foolish men, and slow of heart to believe all that the prophets have spoken! Was it not necessary that the Christ should suffer these things and enter his glory?" And beginning with Moses and all the prophets, he interpreted to them in all the scriptures the things concerning himself.

So they drew near to the village to which they were going. He appeared to be going further, but they constrained him saying, "Stay with us, for it is toward evening and the day is now far spent." So he went in to stay with them. When he was at table with them, He took bread and blessed, and broke it, and gave it to them. And their eyes were opened and they recognized him; and he vanished out of their sight. They said to each other, "Did not our hearts burn within us while he talked to us on the road, while he opened to us the scriptures?" And they rose that same hour and returned to Jerusalem; and they found the eleven gathered together and those who were with them, who said, "The Lord has risen indeed, and has appeared to Simon!" Then they told what had happened on the road, and how he was known to them in the breaking of the bread.

NOTES

1. John 20:29
2. Matthew 28 : 11-13
3. Mark 16:8
4. Matthew 28:17
5. Luke 24:51
6. Acts 2:2b
7. 1 Corinthians 15:6
8. Acts 1:6
9. Acts 1:7,8
10. Luke 24: 13-35

XIII

JOHN

" THE DIVINE PEN " is the term often applied to the work of John as found in his Gospel. It is a deserved appellation. There is no calculating what this Gospel has meant to succeeding generations. If only one verse of it had remained to us, that verse would have had an impact of heroic proportions:

> *For God so loved the world that he gave his only son, that whoever believes in him should not perish but have eternal life.*[1]

John's Gospel is full of this sort of expression. At the very start we recognize that we are in a different world from the earthy one found in the Synoptics:

> *In the beginning was the Word and the Word was with God, and the Word was God. He was in the beginning with God; all things were made through him, and without him was not anything made that was made. In him was life, and the life was the light of men. The light shines in darkness, and the darkness has not overcome it... And the Word became flesh and dwelt among us, full of grace and truth; we have beheld his glory, glory as of the only Son from the Father.*[2]

What shall we quote, and what leave unquoted?

> *But the hour is coming, and now is, when the true worshipers will worship the Father in spirit and in truth, for such the Father seeks to worship him.*[3]

There are the famous "I am's":

> *I am the bread of life: he who comes to me shall not hunger, and he who believes in me shall never thirst.*[4]

> *I am the light of the world, he who follows me will not walk in darkness, but will have the light of life.*[5]

> *Truly, truly, I say to you, I am the door of the sheep.*[6]

> *I am the good shepherd; I know my own, and my own know me, as the Father knows me and I know the Father; and I lay down my life for the sheep.*[7]

And the immortal:

> *I am the resurrection and the life, he who believes in me, though he die, yet shall he live, and whoever lives and believes in me shall never die.*[8]

The sixth and next-to-last "I am" is occasioned by Thomas' question: "Lord, we do not know where you are going; how can we know the way?" Jesus' answer lies on every Christian heart:

> *I am the way, the truth, and the life; no one comes to the Father, but by me.*[9]

Lest this be taken too stringently, we will return to the thought later.

Then there are such gems as:

> *A new commandment I give to you, that you love one another; even as I have loved you, that you also love one another. By this all men will know that you are my disciples, if you have love for one another.*[10]

Alas, "All men" have not beheld many of his disciples! Wherever it is said that Christianity has failed, it is not Christianity, but Christians.

And there are those great theological truths, borne out by experience, sometimes bitter, sometimes rapturous. One of these comes with the final " I am ":

> *Abide in me, and I in you. As the branch cannot bear fruit of itself, unless it abides in the vine, neither can you, unless you abide in me. I am the vine, you are the branches. He who abides in me, and I in him, he it is that bears much fruit, for apart from me you can do nothing.*[11]

I think it important here to note that there are those who do actually abide in him, but who for one reason or another are not fully aware of it. I remember an old Jewish vaudevillian who was invited one Sunday to attend a Methodist service. He declined, but added, "That wonderful young man whom you worship - he and I belong to the same club."

When ecclesiastics become dogmatic about "channels of grace," as if the church were some sort of heavenly bureaucracy, I find myself clinging to:

> *If a man loves me, he will keep my word, and my Father will love him, and we will come to him and make our home with him.*[12]

Apparently the Lord can by-pass the ecclesiastics, yes, and even the creeds..

There are some remarkable scenes in John's Gospel - scenes characterized by sparkling conversations between Jesus and various types of persons representing different points of view. These include the "private interview" of Nicodemus with the Master,[13] Jesus' encounter with the Samaritan woman at the well,[14] and the drawn-out (and highly intriguing) hubbub over the man born blind.[15] The author had the capacity to "put us there" and to make us feel the tensions caused by the presence of one such as Jesus.

And, of course, there are such words as those immortalized by the King James Version and memorized by generations of those who mourn:

> *Let not your heart be troubled: ye believe in God, believe also in me. In my Father's house are many mansions: if it were not so, I would have told you. I go to prepare a place for you. And if I go and prepare a place for you, I will come again, and receive you unto myself; that where I am, there ye may be also.*[16]

When I die, I trust that someone will read over the grave:

> *All that the Father giveth me shall come to me; and him that cometh to me I will in no wise cast out.*[17]

Having said all this, and said it, indeed, "in summary" (so much more could be added), it is, I think, highly necessary to go on to say that there are problems - serious problems - with accepting the Gospel of John as an historical document.

The Fourth Gospel is a magnificent piece of writing by one who has been deeply moved - moved to the extent that he moves virtually all who read him. It is, I believe, a meditation on the nature of our Divine Visitor - a meditation with which we quickly identify. But serious questions still remain as to its historicity.

The evangelist is obviously aware of the other Gospels and includes a modicum of events found in them also. Before the passion, these amount to references to John the Baptist (but no baptism of Jesus), the feeding of the multitude (once), the walking on the sea, the annointing of Jesus' feet (considerably altered) and the Last Supper (but no institution of the Lord's Supper). Most of the material in the fourth Gospel is peculiar to John, and some of it, like the raising of Lazarus, is given such importance in the narrative that one wonders how it could possibly have been omitted by the other evangelists. More significant than this, however, is the point of view, which is entirely different.

That we are dealing with a very dissimilar Gospel becomes immediately apparent when we find the cleansing of the Temple, which in the Synoptics is given as the immediate cause of Jesus' death, placed not at the end of his ministry but at the beginning. There is no "messianic secret" in John - no waiting for the development of the disciples' understanding. In John, Jesus declares his messiahship at the outset, and continues to declare it throughout the entire sequence. In Chapter One, Nathanael says to him, "Rabbi, you are the Son of God! You are the King of Israel!"[18] In fact, in a later controversy with adversaries, Jesus reminds them that he had told them who he was "from the beginning."[19]

The cleansing of the Temple, which was a messianic act, is thus removed as the immediate cause of the crucifixion, which means that the passion must be precipitated by another event, which John designates as the raising of Lazarus - an event not even mentioned in the Synoptics. Thus the "Palm Sunday" episode, which in the other Gospels constituted Jesus' first public announcement of his messiahship - and which drew the appropriate response - in John is the result of his fame for raising Lazarus. John adds that only later did the disciples think of the prophecy in Zechariah. In the meantime, John tells of how the authorities wanted to kill Lazarus - a somewhat illogical urge under the circumstances. But getting rid of Jesus before the crowd made him a king and thereby stirred up the Romans is given by John as the main intent of the council, the disruption in the Temple having faded into the past. This also gave John his opportunity to voice his doctrine of the atonement, which he does through the words of the High Priest: "You know nothing at all; you do not understand that it is expedient for you that one man should die for the people, and that the whole nation should not perish."[20]

Hence, the holding of the Temple by Jesus is not even mentioned, the bravery of the Master is obscured, Gethsemane is glossed over - referred to only as the place of betrayal - and Jesus goes through the passion as one who simply must go through another bad day before coming out on top.

Which brings us hard against the fact that John attributes divine foreknowledge to Jesus, thus coming dangerously close to denying him his humanity. "Then Jesus," he writes of the betrayal, "knowing all that was to befall him, came forward ..."[21] Suddenly we find ourselves in a passion play. One even gets the impression that Judas, who in the Synoptics betrays Jesus for very human reasons, in John betrays him because he had been chosen to do so. "For Jesus knew from the first," John writes in Chapter Six, "who those were that did not believe, and who it was that should betray him."[22] Indeed, Jesus is quoted as early characterizing Judas as "a devil"[23] - hardly the attitude of someone who chose a man to bring him on. Our sympathies tend to move toward Judas!

The Gospel of John definitely reveals the influence of controversies much later than the time of Jesus. This comes out most clearly in the repeated references to "the Jews" as Jesus' opponents. "The Jews then murmured at him."[24] "Rabbi, the Jews were but now seeking to stone you."[25] The disciples hid themselves "for fear of the Jews."[26] In the Synoptics Jesus is opposed by scribes, Pharisees and Sadducees, but not by "the Jews." The reason is obvious: they were all Jews. Jesus, his disciples, his friends as well as his foes: all were Jews. If Jesus regarded himself as anything, it was as a Jew - as one who fulfilled the Law and the Prophets - a Jew of Jews. All of his concepts were Jewish, all of his foundations. The synagogue was his podium, the Temple, his cathedral.

John's Gospel came along after the cleavage - a cleavage which the Jesus of the Synoptics sought desperately to avoid. Matthew records the Master as exclaiming:

> *Oh Jerusalem, Jersualem, killing the prophets and stoning those who are sent to you! How often would I have gathered your children together as a hen gathers her brood under her wings, and you would not!*[27]

While there was certainly no intent of anti-Semitism in the mind of the evangelist, the Johannine passages about "the Jews" have been a source of enormous embarrassment to good Christian people living in Jewish communities. It is all very well to say that the Jews rejected Jesus, but what about the thousands who did not reject him? And what of later generations of Jewish people who themselves were so rejected and persecuted by so-called Christians that accepting Jesus as the Christ became an emotional impossibility to them?

In this regard we must also admit that in John's Gospel Jesus is depicted not only as arguing with "the Jews," but also as actually baiting them:

> *Jesus said to them* [the Jews], *"If God were your Father, you would love me, for I proceeded and came forth from God; I came not of my own accord, but he sent me. Why do you not understand what I say? It is because you cannot bear to hear my word. You are of your father the devil. He was a murderer from the beginning, and has nothing to do with the truth, because there is no truth in him. When he lies, he speaks according to his own nature, for he is a liar and the father of lies. But, because I tell the truth, you do not believe me."*[28]

In the Synoptics, Jesus has harsh words for hypocrites, but never for "the Jews." I, for one, cannot believe that Jesus ever spoke this way to anyone.

Another striking difference between John and the other Gospels has to do with the matter of "signs." We have already noted how in the Synoptics Jesus is repeatedly asked by his adversaries to give a sign from Heaven, and how he repeatedly refused to do so. The only sign which he was willing to offer was "the sign of Jonah" - the testimony of his own words and life. To decide his status from these, he most definitely left to us.

In John, however, the exact opposite prevails. "Yet many people believed in him," the evangelist states; "they said, 'When the Christ appears, will he do more signs than this man has done?'"[29] The Synoptic writers would not have considered this as adequate grounds for belief in Jesus. But the Jesus of John begins by turning water into wine to "manifest his glory,"[30] and ends by deliberately letting Lazarus die so that he could raise him "that they may believe that thou didst send me."[31]

That Jesus did not give the ultimate sign by coming down from the cross is explained by John in Jesus' words: "for this reason, the Father loves me, because I lay down my life, that I may take it again. No one takes it from me, but I lay it down of my own accord ..."[32] Again, we are dealing with John's doctrine of the atonement, so that Jesus can say (during his final week in Jerusalem), "Now is my soul troubled. And what shall I say, 'Father, save me from this hour?' No, for this purpose I have come to this hour"[33] - a very different story from the Synoptics' version of the prayer in the garden: "Abba, Father, all things are possible to thee; remove this cup from me; yet not what I will, but what thou wilt."[34]

In all clarity, it must be pointed out here that John's doctrine of the atonement had little resemblance to later versions of that controversial tenet. His view of the reason for Jesus' death was simply that it was "to gather into one the children of God who are scattered abroad."[35] Or, as he quotes Jesus himself, "I, when I am lifted up from the earth, will draw all men to myself."[36] He also strove to identify Jesus with the Paschal Lamb, sacrificed in the Temple at the Passover.[37] Still, Jesus' death was to John exactly what it was to the other Gospel writers: the ultimate expression of love, and thus of forgiveness, and at such a price. The "Johannine problem" lies in John's apparent incapacity to let Jesus be Jesus.

Which brings us to another marked difference between John and the Synoptics.

The Jesus of the first three Gospels is a supremely non-theological teacher. Before his arrival in Jerusalem, the closest that he ever gets to referring to himself in theological terms is found in one passage in Matthew (and its parallel in Luke):

> *All things have been delivered to me by my Father; and so no one knows the Father except the Son and anyone to whom the Son chooses to reveal him. Come to me, all who labor and are heavy-laden, and I will give you rest. Take my yoke upon you, and learn from me; for I am gentle and lowly in heart, and you will find rest for your souls. For my yoke is easy, and my burden light."*[38]

For the balance, Jesus' teachings in the Synoptics, as we have seen, deal with faith, forgiveness, love and humility. They have to do with us, not with him. The famous sermon treats with nothing else. There is a good deal in the Synoptics about the meaningless burdens of the Law, and there are parables. "With many such parables," says Mark, "he spoke the word to them, as they were able to hear it; he did not speak to them without a parable, but privately to his own disciples he explained everything."[39]

In contrast to the plethora of parables in the Synoptics, John has not a single one - an arresting divergence, to say the least. We have long soliloquies with his Father (Who heard these?), all having to do with his relationship with the Father and with his followers. The theology reflects the deep thinking about Christ and the Trinity in which the early church was then engaged, but it certainly does not reflect the Jesus found in the first three Gospels. We even find ourselves with a Christ who prays for his followers but *not* for "the world"[40] - a rather different emphasis from that of the shepherd who leaves the ninety-nine sheep to go and search for the lost one.[41]

John, of course, was dealing with the rise of heresies: "John the Baptist was more of a prophet than Jesus;" "Jesus was Son of God only from his baptism until before his death;" "Jesus was divine but not human;" "Jesus was human but not divine;" "Jesus was not the Messiah;" etc., etc. John's theology was hammered out on the anvil of controversy. He did, I believe, extraordinarily well, but in so doing, he came close to destroying the historic Jesus. Had he put his thoughts into the form of an epistle, we would have been the gainers. The three brief epistles which he did give us are superb, yet even here we run into the same hard line towards those who disagree:

> *Who is a liar but he who denies that Jesus is the Christ?*[42]

This, of course, is the basis of his harshness towards "the Jews" and of the references in his Gospel to Jesus as the only way to the Father. Theologically, Christians believe this, but in practice they must recognize that God Almighty - Father, Son and Holy Spirit - has ways of reaching people before people reach him. To go around condemning non-believers is not the Christian way. If it were, Jesus Christ himself would never have gone to the cross.

Who then was this John? Was he one of the twelve? The references to "the disciple whom Jesus loved," of which there are five in the Gospel, are generally taken as the signature of the author. There are many of us who do not care for these references to begin with. They seem out of place with a man like Jesus. Favoritism hardly appears as an appropriate arrow in his quiver. More than likely the references are intended to enhance the stature of the Gospel, implying that it was written by that disciple (who thus had "inside knowledge") or by a disciple of that disciple.

Whoever wrote the Gospel of John was obviously dissatisfied with the Synoptics' picture of a Messiah who was "gentle and lowly in heart." He therefore rewrote the whole story, so emphasizing Jesus' divinity that he all but destroyed his humanity. This, I believe, is the reason for the insertion into the narrative of such notations as "Jesus wept"[43] and "I thirst"[44] - necessary adjuncts to bolster a rapidly disappearing manhood. Yet even the thirst item has to be explained as fulfilling scripture. Imagine!

We all love the Gospel of John. In spite of its "tough line" and total lack of a developing human drama, it offers us much that is beautiful, moving and patently inspired. But is it history? I rather hope not. Personally, I far prefer the down-to-earth man of the Synoptic Gospels: the lowly man who was born in a stable, worked in a carpenter's shop and ultimately trudged the dusty lanes of Galilee. Somehow I respond to that man: the man who told stories, welcomed the children, healed the sick, punched holes in the pretenses of the mighty - the man who sweated blood in Gethsemane, asked his father to remove the cup, and finally died in agony with a cry of despair on his lips. This was real, and this, I hold, was God.

NOTES

1. John 3:16
2. John 1: 1-5,14
3. John 4:23
4. John 6:35
5. John 8:12
6. John 10:7
7. John 10:14
8. John 11: 25-26
9. John 14: 5-6
10. John 13: 34-35
11. John 15: 4-5
12. John 14:23
13. John 3:1-15
14. John 4:1-42
15. John 9
16. John 14:1-3 (KJV)
17. John 6:37 (KJV)
18. John 1:49
19. John 8:25
20. John 11:49b-50
21. John 18:4a
22. John 6:64b
23. John 6:71
24. John 6:41
25. John 11:8
26. John 20:19

27. Matthew 23:37

28. John 8:42-45

29. John 7:31

30. John 2:1-11

31. John 11:42b

32. John 10:17-18a

33. John 12:27

34. Mark 14:36

35. John 11:52

36. John 12:32

37. John 1:29 and 36 (Note also John's timing of the crucifixion to coincide with the eve of Passover, when the Paschal Lamb was sacrificed. This is another departure from the Synoptics, who place the Last Supper at that time. It also may account for John's omission of the institution of the Lord's Supper. He apparently regarded the crucifixion itself as the institution of that rite. He thus emphasized the termination of the need for the Temple rite.)

38. Matthew 11:27-30, Luke 10:22

39. Mark 4:33-34

40. John 17:9

41. Matthew 18:12, Luke 15:4

42. 1 John 2:22

43. John 11:35

44. John 19:28

XIV

APOSTLES AND EPISTLES

IT IS NOT THE PURPOSE of this work to examine every book in the Bible, but only to pursue the sacred writings with a particular eye towards how they help us to believe. In this respect, the Book of the Acts of the Apostles, an extraordinary document written by Luke, plus the Epistles of Paul, Peter, Jude, James, John and the unknown author of Hebrews are indeed helpful. Some are more helpful than others, but all of them show how Christian thought developed in the years immediately after Jesus' departure.

Luke tells us that at the time of Jesus' ascension, as the disciples saw him lifted up, "while they were gazing into heaven as he went, behold, two men stood by them in white robes, and said, 'Men of Galilee, why do you stand looking into heaven?'"[1] The implication was obvious: an overwhelming responsibility now lay on the shoulders of this small, rag-tag group. For us, who take the existence of Christianity for granted, it is all but impossible even to imagine the magnitude of the task which confronted these few men and women. Luke numbers them at "about a hundred and twenty."[2] On this infinitesimal number pivoted what many consider to be the ultimate revelation of the Lord God Almighty.

That these did not long stand "gazing into heaven" is borne out by the amazing fact that within 300 years it was necessary for the Roman Emperor to recognize Christianity as the dominant religion in the empire. But the initial steps were the crucial ones, and the ones of which we read in the Acts of the Apostles and in the Epistles.

It was Peter's address in Jerusalem, after the Pentecost experience with the Holy Spirit (of which more later), that began the movement. The disciples quickly found that it drew the same sort of people that Jesus drew and, likewise, the same sort of opposition. Since the movement itself was regarded by the disciples as nothing more nor less than the fulfillment of the Jewish prophecies, the first issue to be settled was the movement's relationship with contemporary Judaism.

Luke says that following the ascension of Jesus the disciples "were continually in the temple blessing God."[3] Obviously, it did not occur to them that they were anything but good Jews. Their presence, however, was not appreciated by "the priests and captain of the temple and the Sadducees,"[4] and, in particular, their "teaching the people and proclaiming in Jesus the resurrection from the dead."[5] It was not long before the leaders of the movement were in the same roiled hot water that Jesus had endured, and the others of the group, under the same suspicion.

The burning question of whether or not Jesus was the Messiah could hardly be avoided, and the authorities' responsibility for his execution did not help to resolve it. Nevertheless, the acceptance of Jesus began to spread, in spite of stringent countermeasures. It was Palm Sunday all over again. Luke informs us that after Peter's initial address, "there were added that day about three thousand souls."[6] Hardly a bad beginning. Perhaps one of the most interesting facts of that time remains that the soil everywhere was so ready for the seed.

But there were other issues as well, very serious issues, and these soon became pervasive.

The Sadducees' objections in the temple had to do with their own disbelief in an after-life. Theirs was a small but powerful party which held only to that part of scripture found in the first five books. The Pharisees' objections, on the other hand, had to do with the disciples' apathy towards the observance of the *Torah* - the whole body of Jewish law. To many of the Pharisees, this alone would effectively cancel any consideration of Jesus as the Messiah.

I think it important to point out right here that, in contrast to the Sadducees, highly orthodox Jews to this day endeavor to follow much more than the rules and regulations found in the Old Testament law, which are elaborate enough. (One has only to read the Books of Exodus, Leviticus, Numbers and Deuteronomy to appreciate this.) Their rules then, as now, were also found in the *Mishna*, the *Gemara* and the *Midrash*: collections of originally oral laws, commentaries and interpretations - all of them based on scriptural law. These comprise a set of works commonly known as the *Talmud*. They lay down a rigorous code, governing almost every aspect of the life of a pious Jew. Taken together, all of these codes are known as the "Torah."

I think it also important here to recognize that those who devote themselves earnestly to following this incredibly demanding code deserve our admiration for their dedication. We cannot doubt that then, as now, many of them were exceptionally good people, deeply mindful of God and broadly charitable towards humanity.

Alas, many of them were hypocrites, using the observance of ritualistic minutiae and legalistic trivia as substitutes for warmth of heart and nobility of spirit. Worse than that, the observance of the Torah in its all-absorbing detail - or even in only part of its detail, such as dietary restrictions - only served to separate practicing Jews from everybody else. Thus the universal idea, which some of the prophets espoused and which Jesus supremely represented, became buried under a mass of cultic detail: "the washing of cups and pots and vessels of bronze and beds."[7]

Since this was the generally accepted Jewish standard of the time (the Sadducees notwithstanding), Jesus' followers found themselves faced with the great big question of what to do about it. And this is where we encounter one of the most astounding miracles in the New Testament, namely, the conversion of St. Paul. Here was a Pharisee who had gone to the extremes of orthodoxy, and who in his zeal had determined to stamp out the new movement. (Irony!) If anyone understood the Torah and its demands, it was Saul of Tarsus (later Paul). If there was anyone who could speak the language of the orthodox, it was this man. Hence, as Luke relates it, while Paul was journeying to Damascus to arrest more followers of Jesus, "a light from heaven flashed about him. And he fell to the ground and heard a voice saying to him, 'Saul, Saul, why do you persecute me?'"[8] What had been going on inside this person is indicated by what the voice added: "It hurts you to kick against the goads."[9] Presumably, Paul's experiences with the people whom he had been pursuing, and especially with Stephen, to whose death he had consented, had ultimately had on him a devastating effect.

Thus in Paul the early Christians gained an advocate, interpreter and defender second to none. They also gained a missionary of boundless energy and consuming zeal. Moreover, Christians as a body gained a theologian whose grasp of the significance of Jesus has served to mould their understanding and form their beliefs ever since. No matter what one's views of

Providence may be, it is extremely difficult not to see in the conversion of St. Paul the hand of divine intervention. The need was acute, the fulfillment superb.

What Paul must have realized was that no matter how many sacrifices one might offer for violations of the Torah, it was virtually impossible to observe its every detail. It was Peter who further enunciated this thought at a conference occasioned by Paul's work among the Gentiles. When Paul sought a judgment from the church in Jerusalem that his Gentile converts might not be bound by the ritualistic details of the code, Peter pointed out that it was making "a trial of God" to put "a yoke upon the neck of the disciples which neither our fathers nor we have been able to bear."[10]

It is true that in his Epistle to the Philippians, Paul countered the attacks of the Torah people by saying that "as to righteousness under the law [I was] blameless."[11] But here he was speaking on a comparative basis vis-a-vis his accusers. Doubtless he was also thinking of the propitiatory sacrifices which he had made in the Temple, sacrifices which not all Israelites could afford.

Peter, himself, had been doing some deep thinking about the whole matter of the code, and had come up with a splendid vision declaring all foods clean: "What God has cleansed you must not call common."[12] This was nothing short of revolutionary.

In the meantime, Paul took up the theme that, aside from the Ten Commandments and their immediate ramifications, most of the Hebrew law, however valuable in previous eras, was of little ethical worth. Echoing Jesus' sentiments about tithing herbs and neglecting justice,[13] Paul wrote, "He is a real Jew who is one inwardly, and real circumcision is a matter of the heart, spiritual not literal."[14] The revolution was in full swing.

But Paul had a deep respect for that portion of the law which deals with ethics, and a very definite place for it in his theology: "What then shall we say? That the law is sin? By no means! Yet, if it had not been for the law, I should not have known sin."[15] This brings us to Paul's great doctrine of grace, which, stated far more simply than by the Apostle himself, is that the moral law reveals to us our sinfulness but is unable to change it: that change can only be effected by God himself. This is the basis for Paul's unforgettable line: "... for the written code kills, but the Spirit gives life."[16]

Which brings us to another major point in Paul's teachings the inspiration for which was definitely Jewish. The Temple sacrifices of that day were an important part of the code, and absorbed a great deal of time - and money - from the devout. Paul's point, a point beautifully elaborated by the writer of Hebrews, was that Christ's sacrifice, since it was actually offered by God himself, paid whatever price was necessary for the forgiveness of sins. This is what it cost the Almighty to come to us. As we have seen, the price was real and it was high. Certainly, it more than proved his love. Do we need, then, "the blood of bulls and goats"[17] to win God's good will? Do the children of devoted parents, whose devotion has been proven, need to make payments to elicit further devotion? It would be an affront to do so.

To the Romans Paul wrote:

> *While we were yet helpless , at the right time Christ died for the ungodly. Why, one will hardly die for a righteous man - though perhaps for a good man one will dare even to die. But God shows*

> *his love for us in that while we were yet sinners, Christ died for us. Since, therefore, we are now justified by his blood, much more shall we be saved by him from the wrath of God ... Not only so, but we rejoice in our Lord Jesus Christ, through whom we have now received our reconciliation."*[18]

This means a great deal to many Christians today, but it was aimed primarily at Paul's own kinsman, to whom it would have much more meaning than it does to those unaccustomed to ritual sacrifice. The fact is that there are many other Pauline passages which fall into such a category, and perhaps none more readily than his much misunderstood writings having to do with justification by faith.

Again the "Apostle to the Gentiles" was writing principally for Jews. In order to relieve his Jewish converts of their inevitable sense of guilt for non-observance of the Torah, Paul went back to Abraham, to whom all Israelites turn, and pointed out that "Abraham 'believed God, and it was reckoned to him as righteousness.' So you see that it is men of faith who are the sons of Abraham."[19] He then goes on to underline the fact that Abraham was four hundred and thirty years *before* the law.

To us this use of scripture is not particularly convincing, but not so with the devout Jews of Paul's time. Moreover, Paul's use of the Old Testament is circumspect. He seldom uses a text which cannot bear his interpretation, even if originally it was not intended to do so. The writer of Hebrews, on the other hand, makes outrageous use of Old Testament texts, quoting them so out of context as almost to reverse their intended meaning. (Of that, more anon.)

Paul's doctrine of justification by faith, initially intended to relieve Christians of the burden of the law, has had an immense impact on later generations. Indeed, it had such an impact on his own generation that James (possibly the Lord's brother) felt impelled to write an epistle explaining that Paul's doctrine of faith did not release Christians from good works:

> *What does it profit, my brethren, if a man says he has faith but has not works? Can his faith save him? If a brother or a sister is ill-clad and in lack of daily food, and one of you says to them, "Go in peace, be warmed and filled," without giving them the things needed for the body, what does it profit? So faith, by itself, if it has no works, is dead.*[20]

Martin Luther called James' epistle, "an epistle of straw." This, I feel, was unfair. James was simply reminding the beloved of the claims of "the least of these my brethren."[21] Further, St. Paul, whose writings on love are without peer, would never have countenanced faith without works. Witness his numerous collections for "the poor among the saints at Jerusalem."[22] James was simply counteracting a misinterpretation of Paul's doctrine of justification by faith. It still needs to be counteracted, especially when undue emphasis is placed on creed and formularies.

As a matter of accuracy, it should be recognized right here that Paul's concept of faith went way beyond any such simplistic notion of faith as a mere act of the mind. Wherever we find it alluded to in his writings, we become acutely aware that it involves a profound, living relationship with the Deity:

> *Therefore, since we are justified by faith, we have peace with God through our Lord Jesus Christ. Through him we have obtained access to this grace in which we stand, and we rejoice in our hope of sharing the glory of God. More than that, we rejoice in our sufferings, knowing that suffering produces endurance, and endurance produces character, and character produces hope, and hope does not disappoint us, because God's love has been poured into our hearts through the Holy Spirit which has been given to us.*[23]

Much more than intellectual, or even emotional assent! We are dealing with an all-absorbing process:

> *And we all, with unveiled face, beholding the glory of the Lord, are being changed into his likeness from one degree of glory to another, for this comes from the Lord who is the Spirit.*[24]

Hence I think it proper to state that in Paul's mind faith was actually the human response to divine grace: "For by grace you have been saved through faith; and this is not of your own doing, it is the gift of God ..."[25]

Lest we overlook the immense problem which faced the original apostles and disciples with regard to winning their Jewish brothers and sisters from the iron grip of the law, we cite here a Talmud story of a doctrinal rift between two rabbinical schools of thought. It seems that the majority of a rabbinical court, led by a great rabbi, were opposed by a dissenting but no less great rabbi. The latter was able to summon to his side of the argument no less than the Divine Voice itself. To this extraordinary intervention on the part of the Deity the majority of the court responded, "The law is not in heaven, the law has been handed down to us on earth from Mt. Sinai, and we no longer take notice of heavenly voices ..."[26]

Hence Paul's rabbinical passages in Romans and Galatians - his references to Abraham, Abraham's consorts and Abraham's offspring, etc. These are appeals from the point of view of the law to those under the law: to those who simply will not listen to heavenly voices. Difficult as such passages may be for us to understand, they are almost inevitably followed by passages of high poetry, setting forth the heart of Jesus' significance to us and to all - poetry which has penetrated to the very genes of successive generations. To these great passages are added ones written by others of that astonishing band. To this writer, at least, these do indeed echo heavenly voices. To such we now turn.

NOTES

1. Acts 1:10-11a
2. Acts 1:15b
3. Luke 24:53b
4. Acts 4:1b
5. Acts 4:2
6. Acts 2:41
7. Mark 7:4b
8. Acts 9:3b-4
9. Acts 26:14b
10. Acts 15:10
11. Philippians 3:6b
12. Acts 11:9
13. Luke 11:42
14. Romans 2:29a
15. Romans 7:7
16. 2 Corinthians 3:6b
17. Hebrews 10:4
18. Romans 5:6-9,11
19. Galatians 3:6-7
20. James 2:14-17
21. Matthew 25:40
22. Romans 15:26b
23. Romans 5:5-1
24. 2 Corinthians 3:18
25. Ephesians 2:8
26. The New Encyclopedia Britannica, 15th Ed., Vol. 25, pp 729-730

XV

TO ALL PEOPLE

"NOW THERE WERE DWELLING in Jerusalem Jews, devout men from every nation under heaven."[1] So writes St. Luke in telling of a certain Day of Pentecost, the day when the disciples (it is not clear which ones) were overwhelmed by the Holy Spirit, and "began to speak in other tongues, as the Spirit gave them utterance."[2] the narrative continues in Luke's inimitable style:

> *And at this sound the multitude came together, and they were bewildered, because each one heard them speaking in his own language. And they were amazed and wondered, saying, "Are not all these who are speaking Galileans? And how is it that we hear, each of us in his own native language? Parthians and Medes and Elamites and residents of Mesopotania, Judea and Cappodocia, Pontus and Asia, Phrygia and Pamphylia, Egypt and the parts of Libya belonging to Cyrene, and visitors from Rome, both Jews and proselytes, Cretans and Arabians, we hear them telling in our own tongues the mighty works of God." And all were amazed and perplexed, saying to one another, "What does this mean?" But others mocking said, "They are filled with new wine."*[3]

It is to be noted here that, whether Parthians or Medes or Elamites, the hearers were all Jews or their proselytes. Yet the seed had been sown: this was to be a world-wide movement, just as Jesus had said. Another seed had been sown: the language of love is universal.

There was still no rift with Judaism, and there was yet hope that there would be none. The beloved were preaching a Jewish religion, and Peter, in his speech that day, leaned heavily on the Jewish scriptures to make his points and win his three thousand. St. Paul, perhaps the most liberated of the Apostles, went to the Jews to the very end. In fact, the last act of which we read in Acts is St. Paul's calling together the local leaders of the Jews in Rome.[4] In each instance some were convinced by him and some not. This, indeed, was the story of the movement everywhere.

The idea of going to the Gentiles was not one which came naturally to the disciples, in spite of all that had gone before. Peter, when he was impelled by the Holy Spirit to visit the home of Cornelius, a Roman centurion, was utterly amazed when the same Holy Spirit "fell on" his hearers.[5] Likewise "the apostles and brethren who were in Judea" were astounded when they heard that "the Gentiles also had received the word of God."[6]

With Paul, the story of going to the Gentiles is somewhat similar. Again, Luke relates:

> *Now those who were scattered because of the persecution that arose over Stephen traveled as far as Phoenicia and Cyprus and Antioch, speaking the word to none except Jews. But there were some of them, men of Cyprus and Cyrene, who on coming to Antioch spoke to the Greeks also, preaching the Lord Jesus. And the hand of the Lord was with them, and a great number that believed turned to the Lord. News of this came to the ears of the church in Jerusalem, and they sent Barnabas to Antioch. When he came and saw the grace of God, he was glad; and he exorted them*

> *all to remain faithful to the Lord with stedfast purpose; for he was a good man, full of the Holy Spirit and of faith. And a large company was added to the Lord. So Barnabas went to Tarsus to look for Saul; and when he had found him, he brought him to Antioch. For a whole year they met with the church, and taught a large company of people; and in Antioch the disciples were for the first time called Christians.*[7]

Obviously, there were many Gentiles involved here, and from then on Paul was involved with Gentiles. This is what ultimately led to the historic conference in Jerusalem, alluded to in the previous chapter, and the momentous decision that Gentile converts should not be bound by the strictures of Judaism. Thus a brand new audience was opened to the preaching of "the word," an audience of limitless numbers and, apparently, few prejudices. To this audience the beloved became more and more committed.

Alas, this more than anything else precipitated the rift with Judaism. Not observing the Torah in all of its detail was mainly controversial. Plenty of Jews did not. Even the messiahship of Jesus was arguable, as the Pharisee, Gamaliel, suggested to his colleagues in the Jewish Sanhedrin.[8] But turning to the Gentiles was unforgivable.

Years later, when Paul, still determined to win his own people, paid what turned out to be his final visit to Jerusalem, he managed to get a hearing before an otherwise hostile crowd. Luke reports that the throng listened intently, that is, until he mentioned his being sent to the Gentiles.[9] From that moment on, Paul was in such trouble that he finally had to "appeal to Caesar," i.e., ask to be tried in Rome.[10]

Making proselytes of Gentiles was permissable, provided they submitted to a stringent observance of the Torah, but accepting Gentiles as such, which Paul had obviously been doing, was beyond the pale. Not only was religion involved here, but also nation; not only nation, but also kindred. It was a case of "we vs. them" to the third power. The assemblage at Jerusalem "cried out and waved their garments and threw dust into the air."[11]

In the meantime, "the word" had begun to spread through the Empire. St. Paul's amazing travels (all carefully chronicled by St. Luke, who accompanied Paul on most of them) were effective in the extreme. Moreover, that many other disciples were also carrying the new faith far and wide is more than evident from the accounts in Acts and from the references in the Epistles and Revelation.

The Empire provided an open platform. It was an arena of many religions, most of them extraordinarily superficial: "rabbit's foot religions." Their tongue-in-cheek followers took them largely with great big grains of salt. Into such a theatre came this small, dedicated band of humble, earnest people, preaching a magnificent faith. One can well imagine the impact of such a noble conviction upon souls nurtured on Jupiter, Juno, Mars, Venus and the like. Such gods and goddesses offered absolutely nothing to those who yearned for ideas and ideals which they could respect and love: ideas and ideals which would give meaning to their lives. And here is exactly where Paul and his colleagues excelled.

Imagine how a thoughtful person, surrounded by a sea of selfish deities, would react to a passage like this one from St. Paul's Epistle to the Philippians:

> *Have this mind among yourselves, which you have in Christ Jesus, who, though he was in the form of God, did not count equality with God a thing to be grasped, but emptied himself, taking the form of a servant, being born in the likeness of men. And being found in human form he humbled himself and became obedient unto death, even death on a cross. Therefore God has highly exalted him and bestowed on him the name which is above every name, that at the name of Jesus every knee should bow, in heaven and on earth and under the earth, and every tongue confess that Jesus Christ is Lord, to the glory of God the Father.*[12]

Or, from the same glowing letter:

> *Finally, brethren, whatever is true, whatever is honorable, whatever is just, whatever is pure, whatever is lovely, whatever is gracious, if there is any excellence, if there is anything worthy of praise, think about these things.*[13]

If one reads the history of the Roman Empire, with all the decadence and savagery of its politics, one can readily understand how a breath of Heaven would be found in John's first Epistle:

> *Beloved let us love one another; for love is of God, and he who loves is born of God and knows God. He who does not love does not know God; for God is love. In this the love of God was made manifest among us, that God sent his only Son into the world, so that we might live through him. In this is love, not that we loved God but that he loved us and sent his Son to be the expiation for our sins. Beloved, if God so loved us, we also ought to love one*

> *another. No man has ever seen God; if we love one another, God abides in us and his love is perfected in us.*[14]

To those in search of true riches, Peter contributed this gem:

> *Humble yourselves therefore under the mighty hand of God, that in due time he may exalt you. Cast all your anxieties on him, for he cares about you. Be sober, be watchful. Your adversary the devil prowls around like a roaring lion, seeking someone to devour. Resist him, firm in your faith, knowing that the same experience of suffering is required of your brotherhood throughout the world. And after you have suffered a little while, the God of all grace, who has called you to his eternal glory in Christ, will himself restore, establish, and strengthen you. To him be dominion for ever and ever. Amen.*[15]

For those who rose to the ideals of the Gospel, so different from the dog-eat-dog mores of Pagan society, there was always the problem of how to withstand the "peer pressure" of the times. This is a problem which is with us yet, and, presumably, always will be. Thus in a civilization held together by the force of Roman arms, we can quickly appreciate the power of Paul's word to the Ephesians:

> *Finally, be strong in the Lord and in the strength of his might. Put on the whole armor of God, that you may be able to stand against the wiles of the devil. For we are not contending against flesh and blood, but against the principalities, against the powers, against the world rulers of this present darkness, against the spiritual hosts of wickedness in the heavenly places. Therefore take the*

whole armor of God, that you may be able to withstand in the evil day, and having done all, to stand. Stand therefore, having girded your loins with truth, and having put on the breastplate of righteousness, and having shod your feet with the equipment of the gospel of peace; above all taking the shield of faith, with which you can quench all the flaming darts of the evil one. And take the helmet of salvation, and the sword of the Spirit, which is the word of God.[16]

Even a letter written primarily for Jews could hardly have failed to appeal to Gentiles when they read (from Hebrews):

In many and various ways God spoke of old to our fathers by the prophets; but in these last days he has spoken to us by a Son, whom he appointed heir of all things, through whom also he created the world. He reflects the glory of God and bears the very stamp of his nature, upholding the universe by the word of his power. When he had made purification for sins, he sat down at the right hand of the Majesty on high, having become as much superior to angels as the name he has obtained is more excellent than theirs. For to what angel did God ever say, "Thou art my Son, today I have begotten thee"?[17] *Or again, "I will be to him a father, and he shall be to me a son."?*[18]

Here is where we encounter the unknown author's rather free use of scripture. The last verse quoted is taken from 2 Samuel 7:14, and refers to Solomon. The Lord is telling Samuel to instruct David as to the coming glory of David's child. We should note that the Lord adds, "When he commits iniquity, I will chasten him with the rod of men ..." Having applied the first half of the verse to Jesus, the writer of Hebrews conveniently omitted the second. No matter, the Hebrews apparently were used to this sort of thing, and the Gentiles undoubtedly considered the quote beautiful. Indeed, no one can consider the Epistle to the Hebrews as anything but beautiful.

Both Jews and Gentiles, familiar as they must have been with priests of one sort or another, would certainly have risen to a passage like this:

> *Since, then, we have a great high priest who has passed through the heavens, Jesus, the Son of God, let us hold fast our confession. For we have not a high priest who is unable to sympathize with our weaknsses, but one who in every respect has been tempted as we are, yet without sinning. Let us then with confidence draw near to the throne of grace, that we may receive mercy and find grace to help in time of need.*[19]

It is from Hebrews, indeed, that we have that memorable line:

> *Now faith is the assurance of things hoped for, the conviction of things not seen.*[20]

and many other beauties redolent of a lofty plain. Jewels appear throughout the Epistles. We quote but one more, this one from James:

> *Religion that is pure and undefiled before God and the Father is this: to visit orphans and widows in their affliction, and to keep oneself unstained from the world.*[21]

One final item must be noted: in the Epistles we find the emergence of the doctrine of the Trinity. Not once is it mentioned explicitly, and yet it is implicit throughout. Jesus' emphasis on God as "our Father" is echoed time and again: "And because you are sons," wrote St. Paul to the Galatians, "God has sent the Spirit of his Son into our hearts, crying, 'Abba! Father!'"[22] But here we have the Trinity: the Father who is, the Son who came and the Spirit who comes. Paul will speak in one place of receiving the Spirit,[23] and in another of having Christ within us.[24] Over and over we encounter both expressions: a loose equating of Christ and the Spirit. We also encounter the idea of having access "in one Spirit to the Father,"[25] the Father, indeed, "who is above all and through all and in all."[26]

The evident interchangeability of the persons, Father, Son and Holy Spirit, has resulted in the famous doctrine known as the doctrine of the Trinity: the teaching that God is one in three and three in one. The classic formula appears only once in the entire New Testament: in the final verses of the Gospel of Matthew:

> *And Jesus came and said to them, "All authority in heaven and on earth has been given to me. Go therefore and make disciples of all nations, baptizing them in the name of the Father and of the Son and of the Holy Spirit, teaching them to observe all that I have commanded you; and lo, I am with you always, to the close of the age."*[27]

Christians, then, should not think of the doctrine of the Trinity as some abstract, involved theological dogma, understandable to scholars only, as in fact it later became in some quarters. Actually, it was the natural outcome of the first Christians' experience of the Deity. If anyone wishes to make more of it, as some have certainly done, she or he is at liberty to do so, but the disciples' beliefs did not come from theological academies: they came from reality. It was this that provided the ultimate power to the religion which swept across the western world.

And we should add that Father, Son and Holy Spirit do speak of something universal, something which all people everywhere at least occasionally sense, and sense as being at the heart of all that is. The Father speaks of love, the Son speaks of love, the Spirit speaks of love. Conversely, every living human being longs for exactly that: love. Were I called upon to read a passage of scripture to a gathering of Hindus, Moslems, Jews, Christians of various stripes, agnostics and atheists, I could read this from St. Paul's First Epistle to the Corinthians, knowing full well that nobody in the audience would dare to object:

> *If I speak in the tongues of men and of angels, but have not love, I am a noisy gong or a clanging cymbal. And if I have prophetic powers, and understand all mysteries and all knowledge, and if I have all faith, so as to remove mountains, but have not love, I am nothing. If I give away all I have, and if I deliver my body to be burned, but have not love, I gain nothing.*
>
> *Love is patient and kind; love is not jealous or boastful; it is not arrogant or rude. Love does not insist on its own way; it is not irritable or resentful; it does not rejoice at wrong, but rejoices in the right. Love bears all things, believes all things, hopes all things, endures all things.*
>
> *Love never ends; as for prophecy, it will pass away; as for tongues, they will cease; as for knowledge, it will pass away. For our knowledge is imperfect; but when the perfect comes, the imperfect will pass away. When I was a child, I spoke like a child, I thought like a child, I reasoned like a child; when I became a man, I gave up childish ways. For now we see in a mirror dimly, but then*

> *face to face. Now I know in part; then I shall understand fully, even as I have been fully understood. So faith, hope, love abide, these three; but the greatest of these is love.*[28]

Basically, this is the gospel which the primitive Christians brought to the world, taking it first to their own people, until they came to the full realization that love, if it is real, cannot be confined to any one group, however favored. As we have seen, their message was like rain on parched earth. Twisted and corrupted as Christianity may later have become in various locales, it was bound to win its way - and for the ultimate salvation of humankind. Thus Jesus' own prediction was at least in some measure fulfilled:

> *And men will come from east and west, and from north and south, and sit at table in the kingdom of God. And behold, some are last who will be first, and some are first who will be last.*[29]

NOTES

1. Acts 2:5
2. Acts 2:4
3. Acts 2:6-13
4. Acts 28:17-28
5. Acts 10:44-48
6. Acts 11:18
7. Acts 11:19-26
8. Acts 5:33-39
9. Acts 22
10. Acts 25:11
11. Acts 22:23
12. Philippians 2:5-11
13. Philippians 4:8
14. 1 John 4:7-12
15. 1 Peter 5:6-11
16. Ephesians 6:10-17
17. Psalm 2:7
18. Hebrews 1:1-5
19. Hebrews 4:14-16
20. Hebrews 11:1
21. James 1:27
22. Galatians 4:6
23. Galatians 3:2
24. 2 Corinthians 13:5
25. Ephesians 2:18
26. Ephesians 4:6

27. Matthew 28:18-20

28. 1 Corinthians 13

29. Luke 13:29-30

XVI

THE REVELATION TO JOHN

ONE OF THE CITY of New York's greatest attractions is a cathedral. One of the cathedral's greatest attractions is its name: The Cathedral of St. John the Divine. Who can forget such an appellation? But there are other attributes equally unforgettable. As one enters this vast edifice, one's eye travels a tenth of a mile down its length to the high altar. Behind the altar are seen eight majestic columns supporting the clerestory above, and behind the columns appear brilliant stained glass windows flashing with scenes from the twenty-first chapter of the Book of the Revelation to St. John the Divine.[1] These alone are enough to justify the book - a book which has otherwise given great difficulties to generations of readers.

Aside from the difficulties, there is a passage in this enigmatic work - a passage which has become one of the foundation stones of Christianity, and which will forever remain precious in the minds of that religion's adherents. The ascended Jesus is quoted:

> *Behold, I stand at the door and knock; if any one hears my voice and opens the door, I will come in to him and eat with him, and he with me.*[2]

What better statement can be found of the basic conviction of those who follow "the Way"?

There is another passage which has captured the imagination of many more than the designers of New York's cathedral windows. This is the passage testifying to the glories of the "new Jerusalem," the city which will finally replace the current evil world. Highly poetic, the depiction transports the reader into a realm not dissimilar to that of music. We quote in part:

> *Then I saw a new heaven and a new earth; for the first heaven and the first earth had passed away, and the sea was no more. And I saw the holy city, new Jerusalem, coming down out of heaven from God, prepared as a bride adorned for her husband; and I heard a great voice from the throne saying, "Behold the dwelling of God is with men. He will dwell with them and they shall be his people, and God himself will be with them; he will wipe away every tear from their eyes, and death shall be no more, neither shall there be mourning nor crying nor pain any more, for the former things have passed away."*[3]

Then follows promises and warnings and a description of the holy city: its walls, its gates (of pearl), its measurements and its golden streets ("transparent as glass"). And, finally this, with its splendid flash of universality:

> *And I saw no temple in the city, for its temple is the Lord God the Almighty and the Lamb. And the city has no need of sun or moon to shine upon it, for the glory of God is its light, and its lamp is the Lamb. By its light shall the nations walk; and the kings of the earth shall bring their glory into it, and its gates shall never be shut by day - and there shall be no night there; and they shall bring into it the glory and the honor of the nations. But nothing unclean shall enter it nor any one who practices abomination or falsehood, but only those who are written in the Lamb's book of life.*[4]

To the credit of many churches, this passage has, on all Saints' Day, usually been coupled with another passage - a passage which provides a dramatic contrast between the glories of the life to come and the humility of those counted worthy of it. We refer to the Beatitudes, beginning with "Blessed are the poor in spirit, for theirs is the kingdom of Heaven"[5] Such is the stuff of glory.

In view of the high drama of the scenes found in Revelation and the artistry with which they are portrayed, it is not surprising that this work is included in the New Testament. But this has not always been so. It was not included in the canon of scripture approved by the Synod of Laodicea (c. 360), the magnificent passage about knocking at the door notwithstanding. (This latter was addressed to the church in Laodicea. However, the rest of the passage was highly uncomplimentary: "I know your works: you are neither cold nor hot ... So, because you are lukewarm,... I will spew you out of my mouth."[6] But three centuries later Laodiceans should have been proud of any such notice!)

Cyril, a famous Bishop of Jerusalem (d. 386), specifically forbade the reading of Revelation in public *and* in private. Alas, there are substantial reasons for this. The book has subsequently proven a great puzzle to some and a real stumbling-block to others. Because of its premises and predictions whole denominations have been formed, parting company with others. In short, there are difficulties.

Perhaps a minor difficulty is the obvious fact that the work, in spite of its opening claim, is not the result of a vision at all. There is hardly an image or a scene which is not borrowed or adopted, albeit ingeniously, from previous "apocalyptic" literature (literature predicting how the Almighty will even scores). If we look in Isaiah 24-27, in Ezekiel, in Zechariah, in Daniel or in the apocryphal book, 2 Esdras, we will find image after image which reappears in Revelation: the dragon,[7] the four horsemen,[8] the sweet-tasting book,[9] the four living creatures[10] (later applied to the four evangelists), the plagues,[11] the sound of many waters,[12] etc., etc.

This, in fact, is one of the keys to the book - an admonition to fellow Christians who were suffering persecutions to "hang in there." The message is that the persecutors will ultimately be destroyed, and that the persecuted, whether they live or die, will ultimately triumph. But the point here is that the book could be distributed among those familiar with the scriptures without the persecutors having any idea of what it meant.

The authenticity of the visions aside, there are major difficulties connected with this bewildering book. Perhaps its having been championed by the great Athanasius, Bishop of Alexandria (d. 373), alone saved it from the fate of other early Christian writings which were not included in the New Testament.

One of the primary problems connected with the book is its plethora of incredible inconsistencies. In chapter five, for instance, the seer writes;

> *And I heard every creature in heaven and on earth and under the earth and in the sea, and all therein, saying, "To him who sits upon the throne and to the Lamb be blessing and honor and glory and might for ever and ever!" And the four living creatures said, "Amen!" and the elders fell down and worshipped.*[13]

This, of course, is perfectly marvelous, but from then on we have chapter after chapter of plagues and catastrophes visited on a consistently defiant opposition until all of such are destroyed and cast into hell. Even then, there is Armagedon, when all the wicked reemerge, in number "like the sand of the sea,"[14] only to be destroyed all over again. Presumably, this lot were not in the throng which included everybody.

But who needs consistency? We are often told only the small-minded. Still, one has to stretch considerably to follow the writer of Revelation. The designation "divine," by the way, is not intended to attribute divinity to the author. It refers to his capacity to divine the future. A better term would be "seer." But his divining of the future gets the seer of Revelation into serious problems.

Feeling the need to give special encouragement to those facing martyrdom for not worshiping the Emperor, he brought forth the prophecy of a millenium after the close of this age: a thousand years when the martyrs alone will be restored to life to reign with Christ. Not that there will be anyone over whom to reign. The wicked will all be in hell, and the righteous, not yet raised.[15] The thought is little short of bizarre. Forgotten also are the words of Jesus as to the rulers who "lord it over" their subjects, "But it shall not be so among you ..."[16]

Which brings us to an even greater discrepancy between the thinking of this seer and the thinking of the Master. St. John the Divine views the present world as hopeless. It is under the influence of that fallen angel, Satan, and the more disasters visited upon it by the angels who have not fallen, the more adamant the wicked become in their wickedness:

> *The rest of mankind, who were not killed by these plagues, did not repent of the works of their hands nor give up worshiping demons and idols of gold and silver and bronze and stone and wood, which cannot either see or hear or walk; nor did they repent of their murders or their sorceries or their immorality or their thefts.*[17]

The only way, then, to have peace on earth is to destroy the wicked. This, of course, is so far from Jesus' mind as to be grotesque: Jesus who taught us to pray, "Thy kingdom come, thy will be done, on earth as it is in heaven."[18] Jesus spoke of forgiveness, of going after the lost sheep, of loving one's enemies, of the joy in Heaven over one sinner who repented. How can one forget that he refused to call down fire on his oppressors but instead went to the cross?

If the Master knew anything, he knew that one has to bear with people and work with them. This, really, is what history is all about. But Revelation has no sense of history. Indeed, the book is definitely deterministic. At its close, the angel is quoted as saying to the seer:

> *"Do not seal up the words of the prophecy of this book, for the time is near. Let the evildoer still do evil, and the filthy still be filthy, and the righteous still do right, and the holy still be holy."*[19]

In view of such an attitude, one begins to wonder what all the plagues and punishments were intended to accomplish. If one's name did not appear in the Lamb's "book of life" - which was written "before the foundation of the world"[20] - one was headed straight for the fire, apparently regardless. There is only the vaguest hint that one might possibly do something about it, albeit a negative one: the Lamb could still blot out one's name![21] Of course the book itself is a contradiction of all this, otherwise it would not have been written. Why else bother?

Right here it must be acknowledged that determinism, sometimes known as "predestination," was part and parcel of contemporary rabinnical thought, although not nearly as cut and dried as theologians like Augustine and Calvin later made it. Individual responsibility was still assumed, the contradiction notwithstanding. Actually, to speculate on God's foreknowledge and his actions is to trespass on eternity. We who live within the limitations of space and time can have no conception of what it means to live outside them. The finite must ever resist the temptation to analyze the infinite. That is trespassing.

The author of Revelation, like some of his apocalyptic forebears, yielded to the urge to cross the border. Be it added here that it appears to this author that Paul likewise trespassed, twice: once to explain why so many Jews resisted the Gospel (answer: to cause the disciples to go to the Gentiles),[22] and once to encourage his Roman congregation to persist in the espousal of faith over the law (inferring that, being predestined, they had nothing to fear).[23]

To assume that God is all-wise and that he works in wondrous ways, it seems to me, is highly logical; but there we must stop. We still have in our minds the coming, the suffering and the death of a unique person: one whom many of us believe to have been God himself. We therefore resolutely reject the idea that the Via Dolorosa was a charade.

God has given us many gifts. As far as we can see, it appears obvious that responsibility is one of them. Perhaps this is his greater gift of all.

A further difficulty with Revelation is the simple fact that it is filled with hate. The woes, the plagues, the bowls of wrath, the fire from Heaven and the fires of hell - these hardly bespeak that love which "hopes all things, endures all things" and "never ends."[24] Not that we judge the writer. Who could remain unmoved while petty officials tortured men, women and even children who would not acknowledge that some degenerate egomaniac was a god? Who would not be enraged when splendid people were nailed on crosses and set on fire for the amusement of a crowd?

Even so, those who remember the Master cannot help but squirm when they read in Revelation that the martyrs cried out to God:

> *"O Sovereign Lord, holy and true, how long before thou wilt judge and avenge our blood on those who dwell upon the earth?"*[25]

Nor do we respond to the pleasure with which the seer announces that Satan and his many followers were "thrown into the lake of fire and brimstone ...," where they "will be tormented day and night for ever and ever."[26]

The seer has, traditionally, been identified with the apostle, John, but since the book can be fairly closely dated with the persecutions of Domitian, c. 92, this would seem unlikely. Further, as we have seen, it is hard to believe that the writer could have known the Master personally. Nor can we accept the idea that the author of this work was the same John who wrote the Fourth Gospel and the three Epistles. Not only is the style different, so also is the Greek. More than that: the point of view is totally divergent. In the Fourth Gospel there is not a single mention of hell. Revelation is full of it.

The First Epistle states flatly, "There is no fear in love."[27] Revelation traffics in fear:

> *But as for the cowardly, the faithless, the polluted, as for murderers, fornicators, sorcerers, idolaters, and all liars, their lot shall be in the lake that burns with fire and brimstone, which is the second death.*[28]

Both the Fourth Gospel and the three Epistles take a dim view of unbelievers, 'tis true, but they leave their fate undefined. Love is still the central theme. Of this precious item we find very little in the hair-raising scenes of Revelation.

Revelation is, among other things, an attempt to solve the problem of evil. It offers an essentially Old Testament solution. The triumph of righteousness is put off to the future. Ultimately God will intervene and prevail. In the meantime, the martyrs will be kept in store for the millennium and the rest of the righteous, for the second resurrection. This is New Testament language, but it is not New Testament thinking. The rest of the New Testament sees evil for what it is: the basic selfishness of human beings. "No one is good," said Jesus, "but God alone."[29] Evil will exist as long as human beings continue to be born. The solution to the problem of evil is not the vengeful intervention of God in history but the suffering intervention of Jesus and of those who follow him. God does not seek to slay the wicked, but to redeem them. He is ever against our sins, he is never against us.

Thus the ultimate intervention of God becomes a person-by-person affair. Society is being constantly redeemed (or it is not). Over and over evil is defeated and over and over it reimerges to be defeated (or not) again. Revelation notwithstanding, there is no God-made millennium, only a people-made advance or retreat, depending entirely on the response of human beings to the Divine Spirit. The battle is not on the fields of Armagedon, it is within ourselves.

NOTES

1. These windows are the work of James Powell and Sons, London, circa 1913.

2. Revelation 3:20

3. Revelation 21-1-4

4. Revelation 21:22-27

5. Matthew 5:3 (See Chapter IX of this work.)

6. Revelation 3:15-16

7. Isaiah 27:1

8. Zechariah 1:8, 6:1-3

9. Ezekiel 2:8-3:1-3

10. Ezekiel 1:10

11. Found in all apocalyptic writings. Note Joel for example in brief.

12. Ezekiel 1:24

13. Revelation 5:13-14

14. Revelation 20:8

15. Revelation 20:1-6

16. Mark 10:42-44 (See Chapter IX of this work.)

17. Revelation 9:20-21

18. Matthew 6:10

19. Revelation 22:10-11

20. Revelation 13:8, 17:8, 20:5, 21:27

21. Revelation 3:5

22. Romans 11

23. Romans 8

24. 1 Corinthians 13:7b-8a

25. Revelation 6:10

26. Revelation 20:10

27. 1 John 4:18a

28. Revelation 21:8

29. Mark 10:18b

XVII

HELL

A FRIEND from New Hampshire once told me of his attending a revival in the East Sandwich Chapel. It was during the last decade of the Nineteenth Century. My friend was ten years old. Members of the congregation shrank in their seats while a fiery revivalist described the horrors of hell. My friend went home in a state of shock. All night long he huddled under his blankets as images of terrifying demons rose before his closed eyes and screams of the damned filled his covered ears. It was many a moon before he could bring himself to walk near a church.

And yet so many good Christian people accept without question the belief in a hell such as this one, the depiction of which all but paralyzed a little boy. It never seems to occur to them what sort of a picture such a credo paints of God.

Is there a decent person in the world who approves of torture? Whole governments are condemned for its use. And what normal human being can long contemplate the continued pain even of the lowliest of creatures? And yet we blandly accept the idea that the Creator of us all, the Deity supposedly exemplified by Jesus of Nazareth, who went to the cross for sinners, can inflict excrutiating agony on his children, however errant, endlessly, ceaselessly and, worst of all, without purpose. The whole idea is positively abhorrent - Dante, Milton and Michelangelo to the contrary. Discipline, yes, revenge, no.

Well, say our hell-minded friends, the fear of hell is a deterrent. But the answer to this thrust lies in an obvious question: Can you cause someone to love God out of fear?

Let us carry the matter still further. The Good Samaritan - would he have been acceptable to Jesus had he ministered to the fallen wayfarer simply because he was afraid that he might go to hell if he did not?

If compassion is what God is looking for, there is little likelihood that he can induce it in humans through wrath.

The parable most frequently quoted by the protagonists of hell gives Jesus' own answer to these very questions. Luke records it:

> *There was a rich man, who was clothed in purple and fine linen and who feasted sumptuously every day. And at his gate lay a poor man named Lazarus, full of sores, who desired to be fed with what fell from the rich man's table; moreover the dogs came and licked his sores. The poor man died and was carried by the angels to Abraham's bosom. The rich man also died and was buried; and in Hades, being in torment, he lifted up his eyes, and saw Abraham far off and Lazarus in his bosom. And he called out, "Father Abraham, have mercy upon me, and send Lazarus to dip the end of his finger in water and cool my tongue; for I am in anguish in this flame." But Abraham said, "Son, remember that you in your lifetime received your good things, and Lazarus in like manner evil things; but now he is comforted here, and you are in anguish. And besides all this, between us and you a great chasm has been fixed, in order that those who would pass from here to you may not be able, and*

> *none may cross from there to us." And he said, "Then I beg you, father, to send him to my father's house, for I have five brothers, so that he may warn them, lest they also come into this place of torment." But Abraham said, "They have Moses and the prophets; let them hear them." And he said, "No, father Abraham; but if someone goes to them from the dead, they will repent." He said to him, "If they do not hear Moses and the prophets, neither will they be convinced if someone should rise from the dead."*[1]

The parable is a classic example of Jesus' reverse humor, and similar in its method to his parable of the dishonest steward (who at least had sense enough to make a few friends),[2] or his remarks to the Canaanite woman (as to his giving "the children's bread" to dogs).[3] In examining Jesus' sayings verse by verse, we often miss their principal points. The point of the parable quoted above seems evident enough: the fear of a hell is not going to deter anyone.

We note the use of the word "Hades." When Jesus spoke of hell, he usually used the term "Gehenna," which referred to the city dump outside Jerusalem, "where their worm does not die, and the fire is not quenched."[4] This had become identified in popular thought with the place of punishment in the after-life. "Hades" (in Hebrew, "Sheol") was the place of departed spirits, good and bad, not only in Jewish thought, but also in Gentile. In either case, the concepts were "au courant" at the time, just as "the hot place" and "the place of harps" are today. Jesus used the terms somewhat indiscriminately, just as we do our terms. The minute, therefore, that we start taking these uses literally, we find ourselves in the same predicament in which my friend in New Hampshire found himself at ten years of age. And this can constitute a real difficulty among otherwise interested people, and a legitimate barrier to belief.

At the start, we should point out that Jesus' uses of the various words for hell are very few in number: in the three Synoptic Gospels a total of thirteen. There are no uses at all in the Gospel of John. There are also no uses in St. Paul, and only one in the other Epistles: Peter's reference to "Tartarus"[5] - the Greek term for the underworld. Paul does have an oblique reference in Romans[6] and, as we shall see, there is also such a one in Hebrews. Revelation, as we have already seen, is the real culprit when it comes to emphasizing the concept of a punitive hell.

I think it therefore appropriate to examine such uses of the idea of hell as we find in the Gospels.

In the Sermon on the Mount we encounter this word:

> *You have heard that it was said to the men of old, "You shall not kill; and whoever kills shall be liable to judgment." But I say to you that every one who is angry with his brother shall be liable to judgment; whoever insults his brother shall be liable to the council, and whoever says, "You fool!" shall be liable to the hell of fire.*[7]

Here the literal-minded will have to set up a cosmogony explaining the position of judgment and the position of the council. Jesus was simply pointing out the origins of crime.

Further on in the Sermon we read:

You have heard that it was said, "You shall not commit adultery." But I say to you that every one who looks at a woman lustfully has already committed adultery with her in his heart. If your right eye causes you to sin, pluck it out and throw it away; it is better that you lose one of your members than that your whole body be thrown into hell.[8]

In other words, it is better to have only one eye than to go to hell with two. Again, to those who choose to take this entire saying literally we recommend a quick trip to an ophthamologist.

There is only one other use of any term for hell in Jesus' conversations. It is an important one because, at least from my point of view, it is so regularly misinterpreted. It occurs both in Matthew and Luke. The Lucan version:

I tell you, my friends, do not fear those who kill the body, and after that have no more that they can do. But I will warn you whom to fear; fear him who, after he has killed, has power to cast into hell; yes, I tell you fear him![9]

Most commentators take it for granted that the reference is to God. Perhaps it is, but I have never been convinced. The Matthian version reads:

And do not fear those who kill the body but cannot kill the soul; rather fear him who can destroy both soul and body in hell.[10]

Both versions immediately add this superb saying;

Are not five sparrows sold for two pennies? And not one of them is forgotten before God. Why, even the hairs of your head are all numbered. Fear not, you are of more value than many sparrows![11]

To me the intent is obvious. Of God's infinite love there can be no doubt. People, however, are different from God and quite capable of assault, battery and murder. Nevertheless, do not fear them, for they can destroy only the body. Rather fear the devil, for he can destroy both body and soul in hell.

(Which raises another tiresome question, namely, that of a literal interpretation of the concept of the devil. I just hope that by now we have made it abundantly clear that our own self-centered condition, when coupled with our natural urges and passions, and who knows what inheritances from primordial times, provides us with devil enough. There is no real need for the creature with forked tail and horns. Such few references to Beelzebub and his synonyms as may be found in the Gospels and the Epistles are, as far as this writer is concerned, all of a poetic nature.)

The author of Hebrews provides us with the only other reference to hell (other than those in Revelation) besides Peter's "Tartarus" and Paul's less definitive one in Romans. As with Paul, hell is not named:

> *For if we sin deliberately after receiving the knowledge of the truth, there no longer remains a sacrifice for sins, but a fearful prospect of judgment, and a fury of fire which will consume the adversaries.*[12]

This, I feel, is overdoing it. I far prefer Jesus' rather literary way of putting it, such as his disposal of the "worthless servant" in the parable of the talents, who was cast "into the outer darkness; [where] men will weep and gnash their teeth."[13]

In the parable of the last judgment, Jesus speaks of the uncompassionate as going into "eternal punishment" but the compassionate into "eternal life."[14] It is a nice distinction: love is living, all the rest is punishment. This is made clearer, perhaps, by the reference to "outer darkness" quoted above, a reference which occurs three times in the Gospel of Matthew.[15] Alas, there can be no predicting that all people will eventually respond to the Spirit. If the will is free, it is free, and therefore unpredictable. Under the circumstances, we can only accept the thought that some may never turn and seek to enter the kingdom of light. To me at least, "outer darkness" is a most adequate description of their fate.

Christ's descent into hell, mentioned in the Apostles' Creed, is a direct reference to his continued search for his lost sheep,[16] or as Peter puts it, his preaching to "the spirits in prison, who formerly did not obey."[17] If the New Testament says anything, it says that God does believe in the second chance, or, to use Jesus' own mathematics, seventy chances times seven.[18]

In spite, then, of Jesus' occasional use of the contemporary terms for a vengeful hell, and in spite also of three references to the concept in the Epistles, we can nevertheless assume that it was hardly a dominant New Testament theme. Such use of it as has been made in subsequent centuries has not served a good purpose in the churches or in society. Indeed, it has, if anything, only fostered a certain disrespect for the Christian religion - that it should place any emphasis at all on fear. Be that as it may, this disrespect is hardly justified by the sources.

If Jesus, as we have seen, refused to call down fire upon his enemies on earth,[19] we can hardly expect him to do so elsewhere. His call was ever for forgiveness, his word was ever for loving one's enemies, and his purpose was ever to redeem humanity - the humanity for which he considered his Father responsible down to the last hair of our heads.

To be disturbed, then, by a few verses which appear to say one thing is really unnecessary when the entire scroll says quite another.

The only hell of which we can be at all certain is the hell of living without love.

NOTES

1. Luke 16:19-31
2. Luke 16:1-9
3. Matthew 15:21-28
4. Mark 9:48
5. 2 Peter 2:4
6. Romans 2:6-10
7. Matthew 5:21,22
8. Matthew 5:27-29
9. Luke 12:4,5
10. Matthew 10:28
11. Luke 12:6,7 (Matthew quotes two sparrows for a penny!)
12. Hebrews 10:26,27
13. Matthew 25:30
14. Matthew 25:46
15. Matthew 8:12,22:13,25:30
16. Luke 15:6
17. 1 Peter 3:19b,20a (See also Ephesians 4:9.)
18. Matthew 18:21,22
19. Luke 9:54,55

It should be noted that in Matthew 13:42 and 50, Jesus speaks of the angels throwing evildoers "into the furnace of fire," where "men will weep and gnash their teeth." However, in three other instances in the same book he couples the place of weeping with "outer darkness," and in another with the place of "hypocrites." Obviously, he was using these terms loosely in accordance with the sayings of the time.

XVIII

"NEITHER MALE NOR FEMALE"

WOMEN COMPRISE ONE HALF the population of the earth, and yet the Bible as a whole is notorious in its chauvinistic attitude towards what many consider as by far the most beneficial sex. In Leviticus we read:

> *The Lord said to Moses, "Say to the people of Israel, When a man makes a special vow of persons to the Lord at your valuation, then your valuation of a male from twenty years old up to sixty years old shall be fifty shekels of silver, according to the shekel of the sanctuary. If the person is female, your valuation shall be thirty shekels. If the person is from five years old up to twenty years old, your valuation shall be for a male twenty shekels, and for a female ten shekels."*[1]

Nothing like making it clear!

The New Testament is far less bald, but such statements on the subject as we find within its pages do not encourage those interested in seeing that women receive their due, or men their just deserts.

In Peter's first Epistle we find this charge:

> *Likewise you wives, be submissive to your husbands, so that some, though they do not obey the word, may be won without a word by the behavior of their wives, when they see your reverent and chaste behavior. Let not yours be the outward adorning with braiding of hair, decoration of gold, and wearing of robes, but let it be the hidden person of the heart with the imperishable jewel of a gentle*

> *and quiet spirit, which in God's sight is very precious. So once the holy women who hoped in God used to adorn themselves and were submissive to their husbands, as Sarah obeyed Abraham, calling him lord.*[2]

Just what some husbands do *not* need.

In the Gospels we find nothing on the subject. It was not an issue which Jesus addressed. Faith, forgiveness, love - these constituted the major thrust of his teachings. Aside from confronting the corruption in the Temple, which for him was a religious issue, he did not address the social or political orders of the day. Unmarried, he nevertheless remained a stedfast advocate of the sanctity of marriage.[3] He had many friends among the opposite sex and, we are told, was accompanied by many women in Galilee who "followed him, and ministered to him," and was also accompanied by "many other women who came up with him to Jerusalem."[4]

These women may or may not have been playing the traditional role. What annoys not a few of those otherwise interested in "the Way" is the endeavor on the parts of both Peter and Paul to make of the traditional role, with its Old Testament roots, an absolute.

In Paul's First Epistle to the Corinthians we are confronted with this admonition:

> *As in all the churches of the saints, the women should keep silence in the churches. For they are not permitted to speak, but should be subordinate, as even the law says. If there is anything they desire to know, let them ask their husbands at home. For it is shameful for a woman to speak in church.*[5]

There is, of course, a contradiction here, since Paul elsewhere declares, and in no uncertain terms, that those of faith are free of the law.[6] To him, only the law of love applied. "For the whole law," he wrote to the Galatians, "is fulfilled in one word 'You shall love your neighbor as yourself.'"[7] Nonetheless, in the aforesaid Epistle to the Corinthians we read these even more startling words:

> *But I want you to understand that the head of every man is Christ, the head of a woman is her husband, and the head of Christ is God ... (For man was not made from woman, but woman from man. Neither was man created for woman, but woman for man.)*[8]

When my grandmother felt put down by her sometimes thoughtless mate, she would exclaim to all in residence, "A rib of Adam! That's all I am: a rib of Adam!"

It was fortunate for Paul that my grandmother was not around when he wrote the following to Timothy:

> *Let a woman learn in silence with all submissiveness. I permit no woman to teach or to have authority over men; she is to keep silent. For Adam was formed first, then Eve; and Adam was not deceived, but the woman was deceived and became a transgressor.*[9]

There are scholars who hold that St. Paul himself did not write the letters to Timothy. I just hope that they are right, because this passage, I maintain, is blatantly unfair. In his Epistle to the Ephesians, Paul has a very beautiful passage about marriage which comes close to making of it a fifty-fifty partnership, but not quite close enough:

> *Be subject to one another out of reverence for Christ. Wives be subject to your husbands as to the Lord. For the husband is the head of the wife as Christ is the head of the church, his body ... Husbands love your wives, as Christ loved the church and gave himself up for her ... Even so husbands should love their wives as their own bodies. He who loves his wife loves himself.*[10]

To the Colossians Paul simply writes:

> *Wives, be subject to your husbands, as is fitting in the Lord. Husbands, love your wives, and do not be harsh with them.*[11]

To many perceptive readers of the New Testament, these particular passages present very serious difficulties, and, as far as this writer is concerned, they certainly should. But who said that St. Paul, or St. Peter, had always to be right? After all, they lived in different times and under very different circumstances: so different, indeed, as to be all but unimaginable to us. How can we stand in judgment? But to try now to hold women back from assuming the same responsibilities as men assume would be like imitating King Canute, who tried to hold back the tides of the sea. If the Church, right back to St. Paul, has been guilty of this, I maintain that Christianity has not. Strangely enough, the seeds of women's rights go directly back to St. Paul himself, who saw that "in Christ Jesus you are all sons of God, through faith. For as many of you as were baptized into Christ have put on Christ. *There is neither Jew nor Greek, there is neither slave nor free, there is neither male nor female;* for you are all one in Christ Jesus."[12]

Not every one is quick to apply to one's attitudes that which one perceives with one's mind. It took the disciples many months (and the resurrection) to discern that Jesus had not come to save the Jews from Rome. It took them more months (and Pentecost) to apprehend that the Gospel should be taken to the Gentiles. It has taken the churches almost 2000 years to realize that women are human beings: that they have all the faculties, all the capacities, all the capabilities that men have, except physical strength. Why should they not use them? Yes, they alone can be mothers, but does this mean that they can be nothing else? The idea is patently absurd.

St. Paul himself leaned heavily on women for the creation, maintenance and defense of the Church. The Book of Acts and Paul's own Epistles name no less than eighteen in connection with the Great Apostle, and refer to others, unnamed. Paul minces no words with regard to some:

> *I commend to you our sister Phoebe, a deaconess of the church at Cenchreae, that you may receive her in the Lord as befits the saints, and help her in whatever she may require from you, for she has been a helper of many and of myself as well.*
>
> *Greet Prisca and Aquila, my fellow workers in Christ Jesus, who risked their necks for my life, to whom not only I but also all the churches of the Gentiles give thanks; greet also the church in their house ... Greet Mary, who has worked hard among you.*[13]

To be noted here is the fact that of the couple commended, the woman is named first, as, indeed, she is again in Second Timothy. But there were also Lydia,[14] Damaris,[15] Tryphaena and Tryphosa,[16] Rufus' mother,[17] Julia,[18] Nereus' sister,[18] Chloe,[19] Nympha,[20] Euodia and Syntyche,[21]

Lois and Eunice,[22] Claudia[23] and Apphia.[24] For a chauvinistic misogynist, that is not a bad track-record.

Women have since proven themselves in every field of endeavor, including the governance of great nations: this in spite of the persistence of primeval prejudices and built-in jealousies. If Paul, who said that in Christ there is neither male nor female, failed to live up to his own ideal, it probably never even occurred to him that he could. There were, perhaps, other issues of more immediate consequence facing the Church, and women did as they have always done: exercise more patience than men deserve.

I trust that the Gospel of love and fair play has at last brought about a new estimate of the roles of women in society - an estimate not based on sheer inertia or on downright superstition.

Years ago, I had a parish in Pennsylvania. We had a large choir of girls and boys, plus adults. As was the universal custom in the Protestant Episcopal Church at the time, only boys were selected to serve at the holy table. One day some of our girls approached me and asked why they could not also act as acolytes. I was unable to think of a single reason why they should not, and so gave my assent to the idea. Since I knew of no other Episcopal church which had girl servers, I felt duty-bound to report my plan to the Bishop of the diocese. I was not required to ask permission for such an action, but I was expected to report it.

The Bishop turned my report over to his chancellor, who went rummaging through canon law for some ruling on this earth-shattering move. Since no one had contemplated such a thing, he found nothing in several centuries of ecclesiastical documentation. Finally he unearthed a Thirteenth

Century canon which stated (in Latin) that if no male were available to serve at Mass, a female could be so employed, *provided* that she did not come within ten feet of the altar. In the meantime, some of my good parishioners had risen in wrath at my scheduling girls on the monthly acolyte rota. However, when I read the Thirteenth Century canon to the congregation, there was a gasp, and then a roar of laughter. Opposition was overwhelmed, including the Bishop's.

Restrictions on women's activities are unfair, unwarranted and ridiculous. If even such magnificent people as St. Peter and St. Paul said or wrote things which combined to intensify such curbs, we can only conclude that, by the standards of the Master, they were wrong.

NOTES

1. Leviticus 27:1-5

2. 1 Peter 3:1-6a

3. Mark 10:6-9

4. Mark 15:41 (See also Luke 8:1-3)

5. 1 Corinthians 14:33b-35

6. Galatians 5:1, Romans 7:4-6, 10:4 (key passages in long arguments for freedom from the law)

7. Galatians 5:14

8. 1 Corinthians 11:3, 8, 9

9. 1 Timothy 2:11-14

10. Ephesians 5:21-23a, 25, 28

11. Colossians 3:18, 19

12. Galatians 3:27, 28

13. Romans 16:1-5a, 6

14. Acts 16:13, 14, 40

15. Acts 17:34

16. Romans 16:12

17. Romans 16:13

18. Romans 16:15

19. 1 Corinthians 1:11

20. Colossians 4:15

21. Philippians 4:2

22. 2 Timothy 1:5

23. 2 Timothy 4:21

24. Philemon 2

XIX

IMMORTALITY

IF JESUS, after his death, appeared to his disciples, then the case for the immortality of human beings is signed, sealed and delivered. For whatever his relationship to God, Jesus certainly was a human being. Therefore if one lives, all can.

Far more important than that, however, is the simple fact that we hold Jesus' divinity to be proven by his character. This makes the case for our immortality more than signed, sealed and delivered, because of the obvious intent of his coming to us in the first place: "For the Son of man," said Jesus to Zacchaeus, "came to seek and to save the lost."[1]

Thus in one man we have ample evidence (1.) of God's existence, (2.) of his devotion to us and (3.) of his intent that we should inherit eternal life.

The immortality of the individual, however, is still a tenet in which it is very difficult to believe. The fact that such a belief crops up in almost every culture and in most religions does not necessarily prove its validity. When we consider the treasures carefully placed in ancient Egyptian tombs and then hear of symbolic TV sets and air conditioners being burned at contemporary oriental funerals, all for the use of the dead, we realize both the antiquity and the modernity of the conviction as to immortality. Its persistence throughout history notwithstanding, faith in immortality can easily be put down to wishful thinking. It is a strong palliative against grief over our loved ones departed, and an opiate against the fear of our own departures.

I find it hard to escape the clutches of this suspicion. I walk by the sarcophagus of Bishop Manning in the Cathedral of St. John the Divine, and view the carving of his likeness which is upon it - so like the way that he was - and I find myself thinking, "Do I really believe that he is alive?"

Ashes to ashes, dust to dust - this is what we become. The brain is gone, that remarkable computer which controls everything - and we still live? It is only natural that we should be very much inclined to doubt it. But that is exactly the point: it is only natural. We are, after all, natural creatures, and therefore should hardly be surprised at our doubts, and should certainly not feel guilty over them. But we are also spiritual. This is the crucial item to remember. And how very spiritual we are!

Some of us are nasty, some of us, mean. Some of us are stingy, and some, devious. These are spiritual conditions. Some are placid and rather boring. This is spiritual also. What else? Truth is, many of us are convinced that to find that which is of the highest spiritual value and to adjust our lives thereto is the principal purpose of this mortal life. But that which is almost universally recognized as of the highest spiritual value is unselfish love, and truly unselfish love, many of us believe, is found only in God. Around this fact revolves the entire plot of our existence.

I get rather tired of supercilious attitudes towards belief in immortality. It is so easy to dismiss it as "pie in the sky," or "the cherry on the sundae." I could not disagree more with this point of view. When someone says to me, "I have had all the good things, why should I ask for more?", my reply is, "What good things?" The object of life, as far as I can see, is certainly not to provide oneself with all the comforts and conveniences of this world. Everything in my experience points to very different objectives. It appears more and more obvious to this writer that life is ours for the evident purpose of learning certain lessons, some of which come very hard indeed. These are spiritual lessons, contributing to the growth of what St. Paul called "the spiritual body."[2] One of these lessons, assuredly, is that all of those so-called "good things," referred to so glibly by so many people, are not really that good after all. It takes an ever increasing number of them to obscure the fact that inner peace does not come automatically with affluence.

In all the current talk about "the good life," we discern no reference whatsoever to goodness, no connection at all with understanding, patience, fidelity, loyalty, compassion, forgiveness, love. These are what characterize "the good life," not the selfish acquisition of things, and these are what bring us true joy. Indeed, I would be so bold as to add that life without love is always pure, unadulterated hell.

Perhaps the greatest of frustrations in this veil of tears stems from the fact that when its great lessons do begin to sink in, there is too little time left in which to apply them. If only we knew "back then" what we know now! How many years we would not have wasted, and how many mistakes, not made! And consider the wisdom of ex-presidents! Alas, understanding comes slowly to us: too slowly for us to take proper advantage of it. The Pennsylvania Dutch axiom is on the mark: "We grow too soon oldt, too late schmardt."

But the implication is there for all to see: we are being schooled, groomed for a service which is beyond this brief, transient realm. In the parable of the talents, Jesus speaks of the two servants who had done well with their master's goods as being rewarded not with "flowery beds of ease"[3] but with greater responsibility: "... you have been faithful over a little, I will set you over much."[4] This, I believe, is us, if we likewise prove ourselves.

But there is more to belief in immortality even than that. The fundamental question is this: How real is one's relationship with God? If it is not very, then no amount of argument will convince one that it is unbreakable. On the other hand, if one is deeply involved with the Unseen, no amount of argument is going to shake the conviction of permanence. "For I am sure," wrote St. Paul to the Romans, "that neither death, nor life, nor angels, nor principalities, nor things present, nor things to come, nor powers, nor height, nor depth, nor anything else in all creation, will be able to separate us from the love of God in Christ Jesus our Lord."[5]

It appears indisputable to me that if there is a God who loves us, then there is a life to come; if not, then we are extraordinarily lucky to have this one.

One of the barbed questions asked by cynics is, "Well, if there is a future life, what would we do with it?" Reminiscing about this life, they add, might become tiresome after a while, and as for playing a harp forever and ever, that could become a colossal bore. The answer to this, as to most captious questions, requires no great depth of thought: God managed to make this world rather interesting; chances are, he is quite capable of doing as well with the next, perhaps even better. In fact, I would venture to say that if we knew too much about the Kingdom to Come, we might soon become impatient with the one which now is.

The service of God is the service of love, and for that there are exactly as many possibilities as there are people. And to consider how many ways that there are for people to serve each other in this life is to amplify a thousand times our appreciation of it. Naming but a few, we think of music, art, literature, science, farming, business, homemaking, teaching, medicine, law, visiting, preaching and so on, ad infinitum. The opportunities given us here are virtually without number. How many more, then, in the larger life to come?

Thus it all boils down to a matter of trust. Unfortunately, many people are so constituted that they trust nobody, even the visible, let alone the invisible. The incredible gifts of this life are, apparently, wasted on them. All that is theirs, "from the rising of the sun even unto the going down of the same,"[6] instills in them no trust at all. It is all an accident. (Some accident!)

On the other hand, many have learned that trust in the Unseen Spirit is the one trust which is never frustrated in life. They hold, understandably enough, that neither is it frustrated in death.

We are natural creatures, and, as such, we are inclined to doubt any existence at all once the natural body has been destroyed. And one should not wonder if one does. But we are also spiritual. "If there is a physical body," wrote St. Paul to the Corinthians, "there is also a spiritual body."[7] What we have to remember is that God is spiritual. It would seem rather obvious, then, that we were created for a relationship with him. If that is the case, belief in immortality is the only reasonable belief.

NOTES

1. Luke 19:10
2. 1 Corinthians 15:44b
3. Isaac Watts (*Am I a Soldier of the Cross?*)
4. Matthew 25:21 and 23
5. Romans 8:38, 39
6. Malachi 1:11 (KJV)
7. 1 Corinthians 15:44b

EPILOGUE

"HOW CAN YOU BELIEVE that there is a God?" I hope that I will someday learn how the thirteen-year-old who asked that question has fared. In the meantime, I trust that this book provides a proper answer to her searching query. There is, of course, much more that could be said. I have, however, endeavored to review the major thoughts and events leading to the Christian conviction. We could, I suppose, expand on them indefinitely. But no amount of expansion, no amount of scholarship, no amount of study can ever take the place of Christian experience. If the God of Jesus appeals to us, then we must turn to him not only with our minds but also with our lives, that is, if we wish to know him. There are theologians who know almost everything that has ever been taught about the Deity, but who still do not know him.

The simple fact remains that if the God of Jesus is real, then he is also available, and if he is available, then we have only to avail ourselves of him.

Dr. Wickersham has held parishes in New York, Pennsylvania, New Hampshire and Virginia. He has also held two "exchange parishes" in England. During World War II he served as a chaplain with the United States Marines. He is currently Rector Emeritus of St. Luke's Church, Hot Springs, Va., Honorary Associate of Trinity-St. John's Church, Hewlett, Long Island, N. Y., and Honorary Canon Emeritus of the Cathedral of St. John the Divine, New York, N. Y. His articles have appeared in *The Living Church, The Witness, The Cathedral Age, The Churchman, The New Hampshire Churchman, The Southwestern Episcopalian, The Anglican Digest, Forward Day-by-Day, The Spire, The Salisbury Arts Festival* and various newspapers. He is the author of *The Cathedral of St. John the Divine*, the official hand-book of New York's noted church.

The author is a graduate of St. Mark's School, Southborough, Massachusetts, Harvard College and the Virginia Theological Seminary. The latter institution awarded him a Doctor of Divinity degree in 1967.

END